THE INSIDER

TAX-FREE
REAL ESTATE
INVESTMENTS

THE INSIDER'S GUIDE TO

TAX-FREE REAL ESTATE INVESTMENTS

Retire Rich Using Your IRA

Diane Kennedy, CPA
Dolf de Roos, PhD

John Wiley & Sons, Inc.

Published by John Wiley & Sons, Inc., Hoboken, New Jersey.
Published simultaneously in Canada.

Limit of Liability/Disclaimer of Warranty: While the publisher and author have used their
best efforts in preparing this book, they make no representations or warranties with
respect to the accuracy or completeness of the contents of this book and specifically
disclaim any implied warranties of merchantability or fitness for a particular purpose. No
warranty may be created or extended by sales representatives or written sales materials.
The advice and strategies contained herein may not be suitable for your situation. You
should consult with a professional where appropriate. Neither the publisher nor author
shall be liable for any loss of profit or any other commercial damages, including but not
limited to special, incidental, consequential, or other damages.

For general information on our other products and services or for technical support,
please contact our Customer Care Department within the United States at (800) 762-
2974, outside the United States at (317) 572-3993 or fax (317) 572-4002.

Wiley also publishes its books in a variety of electronic formats. Some content that
appears in print may not be available in electronic books. For more information about
Wiley products, visit our web site at www.wiley.com.

Library of Congress Cataloging-in-Publication Data:
Kennedy, Diane, 1956–
    The insider's guide to tax-free real estate investments : retire rich using your ira
/ Diane Kennedy, Dolf de Roos.
      p. cm.
   ISBN-13: 978-0-470-04398-1 (pbk.)
   ISBN-10: 0-470-04398-9 (pbk.)
   1. Real estate investment—United States.   2. Real estate investment—
Taxation—United States.   3. Retirement income—United States—Planning.   4.
Retirement income—Taxation—United States.   I. De Roos, Dolf.   II. Title.
HD255.K389 2007
332.63'24—dc22

                                 2006015377

Printed in the United States of America.

10 9 8 7 6 5 4 3 2 1

Contents

Contents

Preface

I t is often said that there are only two certainties in life: death, and taxes.

This book presents no evidence that we can overcome the inevitability of death. However, we present evidence that taxes are *not* a certainty. Recent changes in tax law have led to the happy discovery that there *is* a way to apply these changes and *pay no tax on your real estate investments*. Legally.

That's not a printing error, and this isn't an underground book.

To understand why it has become possible to invest in real estate without paying tax, we need to consider two items.

The first item is the complexity of modern-day taxes in the United States. Our Tax Code is currently *five thousand times* as long as the Constitution. It is so long and so complex that even the IRS has conceded the fact that no one person can possibly understand the Code in its entirety. And yet, at the same time, our government is wise enough to recognize that lowering taxes actually boosts economic activity and often results in an increased tax take anyway. This isn't just an American trend. With the globalization of business, governments around the world are competing with each other (through reduced tax rates) to get your international business.

The second thing we need to understand is that the savings record of Western nations has become appalling. With the notable exception of Japan, whose citizens diligently save an average of 16 percent of their income, the rest of the Western world is saving less and less. Indeed, in the United States, we are spending more than we earn, resulting in *negative savings*. That gives the U.S. government an excellent reason to encourage us to save: It doesn't want the burden of looking after masses of old, poor people!

Most of us understand that taxes are a necessary evil. While on the one hand no one *likes* paying taxes, on the other hand we all want to enjoy the facilities and services provided by governments. But something else is going on, too. While most people think that taxes are simply a mechanism to raise revenue, there is a second function: shaping the social behavior of citizens.

Think about cigarette and alcohol taxes for a minute. In 1999, taxes accounted for about 51 percent of the price of a bottle of spirits. Tobacco is even higher—almost 80 percent of the cost of a package of cigarettes is tax. Why? To convince us to modify and moderate our behavior. People who don't drink or smoke are healthier and less of a drain on government-funded resources.

This policy of social engineering isn't limited to alcohol and tobacco, either. The government also uses tax benefits like depreciation to convince us to do certain things. A high depreciation rate on computer equipment may result in some lost tax revenue (as businesses use the corresponding tax loophole to lower their taxes), but it also encourages those same businesses to upgrade their computer equipment more frequently (and pay tax on their purchases). That means a higher demand for computer equipment overall, leading to increased production and (hopefully) a more robust and competitive computer industry (which pays taxes on its income), as well as more efficient and competitive businesses that use the newer computers.

The government has applied the same idea to personal retirement funds. We have retirement-saving options today that prior generations couldn't even have dreamed of. And, yes, by giving people a tax break on their retirement savings the government will lose some money in the short term. But if those savings kickstart a generation of people into saving for their retirement, then it stands to reason that fewer people will need government assistance down the road. And, as the price of everything seems to go up regularly, it makes sense to think that future health and welfare costs will, too. So while the government may lose $1 in tax today thanks to your 401(k) contribution, it will save $5 on the services you won't need in 20 years because you have a good retirement fund and don't need (or qualify) for government assistance.

But before you get all warm and fuzzy and begin penning thank you notes to your senator, let's be realistic here. Many retirement plans are not tax-free but tax-deferred. That means you've got to pay up eventually—which is exactly what the government is counting on. By giving you seeds in the form of investment savings, they can afford to tax the crop later. Make no mistake here: Governments around the world are pragmatic and patient—they can afford to wait you out.

Knowing that, it's easy to understand how, for many, paying no tax is the Holy Grail of finance. People spend thousands—even hundreds of thousands—of dollars trying to figure out how not to pay tax. But many of these expensive structures and tax shelters are dubious at best and downright illegal at worst.

That isn't the case here. This book presents you with simple, perfectly legal, and supremely efficient ways to save for your retirement without paying any (or a lot) of taxes. There are even tips for those of you who've had some hard times, or who've just had life get in the way of your retirement planning. If you're one of those people, and you're feeling hopeless or discouraged, don't. There is still time, and the strategies in this book are so supercharged you can grow even the smallest pension into a comfortable nest egg.

At the end of the day, if you plan to live, eat and vacation well in your golden years, it's becoming pretty apparent that you had better do something to enable you to afford it. A word of warning, however: the ideas presented in this book may become addictive.

Successful investing!

—Dolf de Roos

THE SECRET FINANCIAL PLANNERS DON'T WANT YOU TO KNOW

We have both been investing in real estate, and dealing with taxes in many parts of the world for a large part of our adult lives. One of us has been investing in real estate since he was a college student—and did so well he's never bothered to try and use that fancy Ph.D. in a real job.

We've also been involved in all kinds of other business ventures as well. Various business ventures we've undertaken include owning restaurants, growing grapes, exporting cars to Japan (how maverick!), importing garments, building two successful CPA firms, and a tax and real estate investing education business that exists almost exclusively in the digital world. But even as these ventures prospered (mostly), real estate investments have always remained at the very core of our overall planning.

The reason why this is such a fundamental activity is because we believe ultimately that the combination of real estate investments and proactive tax planning is the most efficient way of making money and keeping it. The IRS and the government agree—real estate is one of the most tax-advantaged vehicles you can invest in, because this is something our government *wants* to encourage us to do.

In Dolf's book, *Real Estate Riches*, he detailed the advantages that real estate holds over other investments, notably stocks. For example, you don't have to pay the entire purchase price up front—most banks will lend you 80 to 90 percent of the sale price, or more if the property is underpriced. You can also buy property below its true market value, increase the value of that real estate without spending much money, and *still* reap the reward of that increased value *without* having to sell the property! And, yes, we have seen the market go up and down over the years, with many people predicting we're in for such a drop right now—but let's be real here: when was the last time you saw a housing market drop to pennies on the dollar? Real estate may flatten or even go down somewhat in value, but you'll never see a dot-com style devaluation.

And it's not like wealth through real estate investing is a secret, either. A significant proportion of the population now invests in real estate compared to a decade ago. The shelves at your local bookstore tell the tale—at the time of writing this book a search of "real estate investor" at Amazon.com reported 501 book titles, while a Google search on the same words returned over *sixty million* hits. That means there are a lot of interested people out there using real estate to grow their wealth. In fact, we're willing to bet that you, or someone you know, is involved in real estate investing, and has probably had at least moderate success so far—if not wild, far-reaching success.

So, here's what financial planners would prefer you didn't know: you can use your pension funds to invest in real estate and achieve far greater returns than you ever will through the traditional investment market. In fact, you can roll over those orphan

401(k) plans you've collected over the years from various jobs into a self-directed pension plan that allows you to make all of the purchase, repair, rehabilitation, rental, or sales decisions on properties that your self-directed plan buys and sells. Even better, if you use the right kind of pension plan, all of the money you make in it can be tax-free. And by that we mean, "no tax." Not now, not ever.

The investing vehicles of choice are the Real Estate IRA (through an IRA LLC) and the Real Estate Solo Roth 401(k) (through a Tax Free LLC), although there are others that will work for you as well. What you'll learn in this book is how to find the one that's right for you, how to set it up, and how to use it. Anyone can do it—there is no income or age limitation—but some will obviously work better for your own financial circumstances than others. One thing is certain: there is a plan for everyone.

The reason this is such a hot topic right now among smart real estate investors is that recent changes in tax and pension laws (some of which only came into effect on January 1, 2006), have drastically increased your options as a self-directed investor. In fact, given the combination of real estate's popularity as an investment and the ability to create tax-free money for your later years, we could soon see a new wave of money pouring into the real estate market.

So knowing that, it's frustrating to have one of the most frequently asked questions we hear from clients and seminar attendees continue to be: "Why is this the first time I've heard this? If tax-efficient real estate investing is the best way of building wealth, why don't financial planners—the ones who are supposed to know all the options and give clients the best advice—recommend real estate in the first place? Why do these individuals recommend a complex combination of stocks, bonds, mutual funds, and futures contracts?" And even worse is their next question: "If my financial planner and banker never told me, is it really legal?"

Let's answer the last question first. Yes, it is legal. We'll give you case law and examples that show you how you can use these laws (that have been around for years) to put more money in your pocket.

The first question, though, is harder to answer: Why haven't you heard about this before? Honestly? Our answer, as simple and harsh as it may sound, is that the financial planning industry has not yet found a way of earning money from putting their clients into real estate.

For example, when financial planners help their clients buy stocks and mutual funds, those planners receive a combination of an entry commission, management fee, switching commission, exit commission, and trailing commission. It's in their best interest to keep their clients active and moving investments around. So, you get a call a few times a year from your planner letting you know that you're perhaps a bit overinvested in one area and suggesting a correction. You say, "Sure, if you think it's best," and your financial planner makes the switch and collects the commissions. If those same financial planners were to tell you about the fixer-upper down the street going for less than market value, they don't stand to make a dime. The day that there is a commission structure for financial planners regarding real estate, they will give it the full credit that it deserves.

That may be a bit hard, and we know it doesn't apply to all financial planners.* But those of you in sales know that when your earnings are based on the type of products you sell, it makes sense that you will try to sell the products that make you the most

---

*There are great financial planners out there! And, through the years, we've come up with a list of ones who understand real estate and include it as part of their client's financial plans. For a sneak peek at our list, please go to www.reirallc.com. Plus, listen in on a special interview with a financial planner to learn what five questions you should always ask when you interview a planner.

money. That's a basic profit-based business philosophy, and most of us who are in business practice it. Despite that, though, we both believe there is still a duty to balance profit with what's best for the client, and it is here that we think many financial planners are falling short, and selling their clients short.

Real estate offers advantages that no other investment vehicle can match, especially when paired with a self-directed pension. Rather than trying to hide this information from a public with a voracious appetite for knowledge, we believe financial planners would do well to embrace it, and figure out a way to profit from it.

Why Traditional Thinking Isn't Going to Work Anymore

Chapter 1

WHY SOME RETIREMENT PLANS ARE FAILING

We have a mutual friend who lives in a gated community with guards on duty 24 hours a day. One of the guards is an elderly gentleman by the name of Sam.

Sam is a pleasant, yet somber character, who has held this job for 16 years. He's in his 70s now—long past the age of retirement—and yet there he is most days, still hard at work. Sam says he enjoys the interaction with people, and we're sure he does. However, we're also sure the main reason he shows up to work every single day, even in the blazing Arizona heat, is that he desperately needs the money. Like so many seniors we hear about in the news and on television, Sam is a member of the elderly working poor, who supplements his government pension with part-time work in order to make ends meet.

So what does your retirement look like?

THE GOOD OLD DAYS

It used to be that all you had to do to secure your future was to go to work for a big company, work hard while you were there, and voilà! You received a pension when you retired. Life was good. All you had to do was land that job, work hard, and you'd be taken care of for life. Those were the carefree days of the *defined benefit* plan.

A typical defined benefit plan was one set up and operated by a business. The business usually appointed a manager to run the plan, and this manager was responsible for all of the investment decisions—good or bad. As an employee, you had no choice what the company invested in—you simply had your monthly contribution deducted from your paychecks or had a contribution made on your behalf by your employer. And, honestly, you probably didn't care what the company was investing in. That's because a defined *benefit* plan is one where the benefit—or the amount you receive each month—is the part that's defined.

The beauty of the defined benefit plan was that you didn't need to care what happened to the money that the company paid on your behalf. It didn't matter how much was put into the account, and it didn't matter how much of a return you received. The benefit was defined, which meant the plan guaranteed a certain amount upon retirement. You received a guaranteed amount of money—regardless of employer mismanagement, or any bad investment decisions your employer made. Any and all shortfalls were the company's problem, not yours.

How much you received was based on a sometimes-complicated formula that considered how old you were when you retired, how many years you had worked for the company or had vested in the plan, and how much you were making at the time of your retirement. But for you, they were easy and straightforward. You worked, the company paid in, and you memorized the amounts you'd receive after 10, 15, 20, or 25 years of service.

But those *were* the days. In today's volatile investment world, returns on investment are uncertain. The explosive growth in the stock market of the late 1990s gave way to the collapse of the dot-com bubble, with losses rivaling those from the Great Depression. Pension plans across the world were devalued by millions of dollars during this time. Inflation is a factor. And advances in health care mean that people are living longer than ever before, drawing from the pension plan for many more years than had originally been anticipated when the plan was set up.

All of these things together have created a disastrous formula for the defined benefit plan. The failing plans you've read about in the papers—Bethlehem Steel, LTV Steel, National Steel, General Motors, US Airways, and United Airlines—are all defined benefit plans. It doesn't matter that they're big, they're running out of money. Bad management, poor investment returns, and longevity of life for the beneficiaries have come together to create a situation where what's being paid in now isn't enough to cover the needs of the previous generation, let alone the needs of the current generation. Companies are taking a hard look at what it will cost to keep these defined benefit plans alive and, in many cases, are deciding the trouble isn't worth it. By declaring bankruptcy (which many companies have done already), a company can free itself from a burdensome defined benefit plan. Other companies have elected to change the rules midstream, and unilaterally switch all of their employees under a certain age to a different type of plan. If you're approaching retirement age, this can be catastrophic—you've worked your entire life believing that when you retire you'll be paid a certain amount each month. And then, with two years left until retirement, the rules change, and you now find yourself in a plan that won't pay anywhere near what you had expected to receive. Even worse, you don't have enough working years left to make up the difference.

At least you'll be in good company. As more and more companies move to dump their expensive plans, people who have worked their entire lives are finding out that they have little or nothing to show for it at the end of the day.

There aren't very many employers offering defined benefit plans anymore. Most employers now offer the defined contribution plan that we describe next. Even if you happen to work for someone who is still operating a defined benefit plan, you may want to have a back-up plan in place.

A Case for a Defined Benefit Plan

One of Diane's tax clients was projecting very high income for their motorcycle dealership and repair business. There were also a couple of interesting anomalies. The dealership's owners were both in their late fifties but all of their employees were in their early twenties. Since a defined benefit plan has contributions that are based on a calculation for the expected pay-outs, it was necessary to bring in an actuary to help out with the numbers.

In this case, a plan was proposed that would pay any retiree a salary of 75 percent of his or her salary upon retirement at 62. That meant the two owners (husband and wife) had only six years left to get their accounts funded. Their salaries were high, and this meant the company had to contribute almost $70,000 into the plan for each owner. Meanwhile, the calculation for the employees showed much lower amounts. That's because the employees were all younger, with more working time left to fully fund their accounts, and their salaries were lower. In most cases, the company had to contribute only $2,000 per employee to meet the actuary's requirements.

For the owners, the defined benefit plan became a great vehicle to put money away and build for the future. It was also a tax deduction against the current income of the company. It was different for the employees. All they could do was hope that the plan would stay in place and keep getting funded for the next 40 or so years.

Diane's firm arranged for a special meeting to be held for all employees to explain the new plan. At that meeting they recommended that all of the employees get very active in planning for their own retirements. Sadly, that's the last thing most 20-year-olds think about, and we doubt they took it to heart.

Remember, retirement plans are a tool for companies to plan benefits with *their* best interests in mind—which are sometimes *very* different from their employees. The same is true for each of us—we need to plan our retirement plans with our best interests in mind.

ENTER THE DEFINED CONTRIBUTION PLAN

A *defined contribution* plan is very different from the defined benefit plan. For those of you who are under 40, the defined contribution plan is probably the only type of plan you've been exposed to.

A defined contribution plan is also set up and maintained by your employer. But the difference here is that instead of guaranteeing you a benefit, you are required to contribute a certain amount. It's usually percentage-driven, meaning that you might pony up somewhere between 5 and 10 percent of your gross salary to the plan. You may even be fortunate enough to work for a company that offers a partial or complete matching option— meaning that the company matches all or part of your yearly contributions. When you retire, you receive pension payments based on the total you accrued in the account. The most common example of a defined contribution plan is a 401(k) or 403(b) plan for government workers. Keogh plans and SEP-IRA plans are other popular defined contribution plans.

Do you see how this differs from a defined benefit plan? In a defined contribution plan, you're making the contributions rather than your employer. You can decide how much you contribute each year based on how much you'll need when you retire, or, as many young people do, based on how much you can afford to put away while maintaining your lifestyle.

What Does It Take to Retire?

Granny on the Porch	60% of current salary
Snowbird at the Buffet	80% of current salary
Bronzed Jet-Setter	120% of current salary

Individual employers offer all sorts of income-to-retirement income ratios. If your plan doesn't offer a high enough ratio, you'll need to do some extra pension investing on your own to make up the difference. Why not aim to be a Granny on the Porch at your Tuscan Villa?

For example, let's say you go to work for a company with a plan that says every retiring employee will receive 75 percent of their salary when they retire at age 65. If you're 25 years old, that means you've potentially got 40 years to pay into the plan toward that magic 75 percent of income number. So your yearly contributions are going to be fairly small, (a) because you have a lot of time, and (b) you probably won't be making as much as senior employees who've been with the company longer than you. But as you get older things will change—remember you're still trying to put aside enough to give you a pension of 75 percent of your salary. If you take a job with that same company at age 45, you've now only got 20 years left to set aside enough to pay you 75 percent of your salary. Yes, your salary is probably going to be higher than that of a 25-year-old (hopefully), but you will also be looking

Changing Plans Midstream

George thought his retirement was set. He worked for a solid engineering and design company with a good retirement plan. It was a smaller company, and he knew the owners, who loved the company and the employees. They promised to always take care of the people who worked for them.

But advancing technology created a whole new set of competitors for the business. It was fighting for every contract and, unfortunately, lost most of its deals to new, overseas competition.

Eventually, and perhaps inevitably, the company went bankrupt. George was now in his mid-forties and discovered how little there really was in his retirement account. Plus, he had out-of-date job skills in a tough employment market.

George had to take a job that barely paid his bills, and faced a choice: take the money in his old pension plan and use it to pay his day-to-day living expenses, or roll it into a new plan to start rebuilding his retirement. If you were George, what would you do?

at making a much bigger payment each month, as you try to make up ground.

Most employers are only offering defined contribution plans these days. Employers don't have to guess how much they'll need for the plan down the road—if they match all or a portion of employee contributions the calculation is going to be pretty easy to make. Whatever goes into the plan belongs to the employees, and that's where the employer's responsibility for your long-term financial well-being ends. There's little or no risk to employers with this plan, either. And if the plan doesn't make any money —if its investments devalue—there is little financial impact on the employer.

TO SUCCEED, *YOU* MUST TAKE CONTROL

So, what's not to love about a defined contribution plan then? Well, how about the fact that you still have a lack of control over how your money is invested. Oh, you might be offered a range of mutual funds to choose from, or even encouraged to invest heavily in your employer's stock, but you don't really have a lot of control over your pension investments. And, whereas defined benefit plans came with a financial incentive for your employers to keep things moving ahead nicely (making up the shortfall), defined contribution plans don't. If the short list of investments you have to choose from doesn't make any money, well that's your problem. If you've overinvested in your employer's stock and it's taken a nosedive, that's also a shame—but hey, you can always join the swelling ranks of senior citizens working as store greeters and security guards.

What we need, therefore, is a way to control our own pension destinies. And, fortunately, we have one—it's just that not many people know about it.

The idea of self-directed pension investing has been around for a long time, but it hasn't been widely practiced. It's gaining power now because our government is beginning to try and educate us as to what we have to look forward to if we don't take some responsibility for our own financial futures.

For those of you who aren't familiar with the concept it's pretty simple: you control what your pension money invests in. There is a *huge* world of investments beyond blue chip stocks and mutual funds, and oftentimes the returns are going to be years beyond the ones you'll see from the stock market. The Phoenix housing market appreciated by over 34 percent between the fall of 2004 and 2005. If you had purchased real estate through your self-directed plan, that would be a spectacular return. Can you say the same thing for your portfolio or savings account?

But self-directed plans can invest in a lot more than real estate. In fact, it's easier to tell you what a self-directed plan *can't* invest in (collectibles and life insurance, and even that isn't always true). And, it gets better: new developments in tax law have led to the creation of a self-directed plan that will pay out tax-free. Not tax-deferred—tax-*free*.

Even if you're not a risk taker by nature, and don't feel comfortable investing in real estate and other non-traditional areas, there's certainly nothing to stop you from investing some of your self-directed pension money into the same mutual funds your employer provides. The returns may be lower, but there should still *be* a return. The point is that only when *you* take control over your pension can you begin to take advantage of new tax benefits that are out there.

Some of you are late to the retirement-savings party, and have probably spent a few sleepless nights wondering how you'll catch up and survive in your elder years. But that's okay. If you've been sidelined from the pension game by injury, illness, family problems, or just a lack of disposable income to invest in the first place, this book may be your map to a more secure retirement in the future and to better sleep at night right now. Believe it or not, it isn't too late for you to catch up and create a decent nest egg. And, if you're young and just getting started, or if you have accumulated a nest egg already, even better! The investing secrets in this book will help you to achieve a future that is safe, secure, and worry-free.

But no matter where you are right now, the time to act on what you'll read about is *now*! Whatever your age, income, savings record, or skill set, the sooner you plan for your retirement, the better it will be. Even if you find yourself in your forties or fifties with little or no savings there is still time—but don't keep putting it off, either.

Are you scared of the future? You don't have to be. Read on to find out why.

Chapter 2

HOW MUCH IS ENOUGH?

Here's an ugly truth. Many skilled jobs have gone overseas to countries where annual salaries are less and the lifestyles are dramatically different from ours. India and China both graduate thousands of well-educated engineers, accountants, and even radiologists each year. Many high-tech jobs that were formerly the exclusive domain of the United States have gone elsewhere. That's not to say that there aren't well-paying jobs available in the United States—of course there are! But the shift in employment demographics has impacted us.

Consider this: the U.S. Department of Labor keeps statistics on just about everything employment-related that you could want. While doing research for this book, we found out a couple of things:

- The food and leisure industry accounts for 8.2 percent of all people working in the United States. The average hourly wage for these people as of January 2006 was $9.12, which equates to just under $19,000 per year (based on a 40-hour work week).

- The retail industry accounts for 11.6 percent of all people working in the United States. The average hourly wage for these workers, as of January 2006, was $12.34, which equates to about $25,600 per year (based on a 40-hour workweek).
- The average hourly wage for all American workers, as of January 2006, was $15.99, which equates to about $33,200 per year (based on a 40-hour workweek).

That's 20 percent of the American workforce involved in relatively low-paying jobs, who are probably spending most of what they earn just to get by. Retirement planning is going to be tough for these people, and Social Security or other government assistance is going to be asked to make up the difference.

With that in mind, if you are not a member of this 20 percent—if you're middle class, upper middle-class or higher, you've got to ask yourself three tough questions:

1. How much will I need to retire?
2. How much have I saved so far?
3. How much assistance will I get from Social Security?

HOW MUCH WILL YOU NEED TO RETIRE?

How much do you need to retire? It seems like a simple question, but the answer is anything but. If you were to do a quick Internet search you'd see things like retirement calculators. These are cute, but really a bit misleading. For example, one we looked at asked the following questions:

a. How much do you make now?
b. How many years do you have until retirement?

c. How long do you think you'll live after you retire?
d. What do you think the annual inflation rate will be?
e. What is the overall return you'd like on your investment?

Doesn't that sound simple? Sure, if you're an economist. If you're not, answering question (d) is going to be tricky. Answering question (c) is just plain morbid, and answering question (e) is going to be hard if you're new to pension and retirement planning. There are better approaches, or at least ones that we like more.

So, how much do you think you'll need to live on each year? Are you happy with what you're making now, or would you like to be making more? Could you get by with less? *Do you want to?*

That last sentence is a really important point. We've lost track of the number of people we've spoken to over the years who are planning to live more modestly after retirement. In other words, these are people who've worked and saved their whole lives, just so they can retire and downgrade their lifestyle—at the *exact* moment when enjoying life can finally take the front and center priority. Yes, they will probably have their mortgages paid off, and their living expenses may well be lower at retirement, but what if they're planning to travel, buy a vacation property, or even buy an RV and travel continental North America? This is our biggest beef with the traditional pension planning model: when you use it, you are *planning to be poor when you retire.* And if that's the case, why bother planning at all?

If you'd like an income of $60,000 when you retire at age 65, and assuming that you earn 5 percent on your savings, experience inflation of 3.5 percent (25-year average) and live to age 93, you'll need a nest egg of $1.327 million.*

_____

*These are non-official, non-actuarial numbers based on our own calculations.

So when you're thinking about this, either on your own or with your financial planner, and someone suggests less than what you have now, the question to ask is *why settle for less if you don't have to?* Because that's the truth. You don't have to. You can even plan for an entirely (or mostly) tax-free retirement. Take a look at your tax return for this year, and imagine what you could have done with the tax money you paid out.

HOW MUCH HAVE YOU SAVED SO FAR?

Now here's a tough question for many of you: how much do you have saved up now? In the call-out box you can see our calculations: to retire on $60,000 at age 65, you'll need a pension worth about $1.3 million. If you're not even close to that amount, you're not alone. A disturbing article we read while researching this book said that China's personal savings rate was about 30 percent of their after-tax take-home income. Americans, however, had managed to put away –0.4 percent of their take-home pay. In other words, not only did we not manage to put away any money, we spent more than we earned!*

But what if you wanted to retire on more than $60,000 per year? The following table shows how much more you'll need to have in your pension if you want a higher retirement income.

If you want to retire at age 65 with a yearly income of:	You'll need to have a pension when you reach age 65 that's worth:
$ 70,000	$1,590,000
$ 80,000	$1,770,000
$ 90,000	$1,990,000
$100,000	$2,211,000

*See http://money.cnn.com/2006/03/03/news/international/chinasaving_fortune/.

WHAT ABOUT SOCIAL SECURITY?

Most of us are used to thinking of Social Security as something we will receive in our retirement years. Even if we have no private pension money saved up, we've spent much of our lives believing that Social Security will provide us with at least *some* type of benefit. After all, we've been paying into the plan for our entire working lives.

The problem with that line of thought is that Social Security is facing the exact same pressures that defined-benefit plans are—more comes out each year than is paid in. Depending on whom you believe, our Social Security system is either in imminent danger of collapse or will collapse within the next 25 years or so without a massive cash infusion from the federal government. And, as the government is funded by you, the taxpayer, what that will probably mean is that your personal Social Security contributions will be doubled or even tripled.

Even if you don't believe all of the doom-and-gloom Social Security predictions, common sense has to come into play somewhere. Consider this: the baby-boomer generation is heading into retirement. This bulge generation, which has strained resources throughout its entire life, is now heading toward the finish line. That means more people will be accessing the same system at the same time than ever before, while comparatively fewer people will be paying into the same system. Instead of a classic funnel approach, where lots of money is being poured in at the top, the wide end, we're looking at an inverted funnel—one with lots of money coming out the wide end.

While no one is exactly sure what will happen in the next 20 years, it seems reasonable to assume that the government will try to look after its poorest citizens first. That could mean lots of things—including some type of phase out of Social Security benefits for higher-income earners, or those with their own pension plans. And, consider this, too: currently the maximum you can receive under Social Security is about $1,500 per month. That's not Bronzed Jet-Setter money—it's more like Granny-on-the-Porch, but the porch sure won't be in Tuscany.

America is not the only country facing a pension crisis. Consider the case of Turkmenistan, which recently overhauled its government-run pension system to cope with dwindling resources. The Turkmenistanian solution involved telling senior citizens that their pension benefits will either be cut back or eliminated entirely. The government there simply doesn't have the ability to pay. Developed, emerging, third world—it's the same story. Countries around the globe are all facing financial crises as their governments struggle to cope with increasing demand on decreasing resources. Some economists and think tanks are even predicting that Western nations will crash economically as their governments eventually run out of money.

The U.S. government (and others) is beginning to recognize the growing problem. We're being given more and more tools to look after ourselves by way of the increasing tax breaks for business owners and real estate investors—because the government is hoping more and more people will get the hint and begin getting proactive about their retirement. On the self-serving side, in almost every Western nation politicians have voted themselves a defined-benefit retirement package that is vastly different (and much more generous)—than the rest of us can look forward to.

What does this mean to you and your Social Security? It probably means that you won't be able to depend on the government to bail you out if your pension fund devalues, goes bankrupt, or you just haven't got enough saved up when you retire. In fact, in all likelihood, your chances of retiring on the government's dime will be pretty bleak.

So, what's your plan for the future, and where are you right now? Are you counting on the lottery to make your golden years golden? Believe it or not, according to two recent surveys conducted by the Opinion Research Corporation for the Consumer Federation of America and the Financial Planning Association, 21 percent of Americans (38 percent of whom have incomes less than $25,000) believe that winning the lottery is the only way they'll be able to accumulate enough for their retirement.

Have you taken your parents' route, working the long-term job in the public or private sector that comes with a vested company or government pension? (And if you are, has this chapter made you nervous?) Or are you, like so many people, trying to save where you can, when you can, and hoping things will work out somehow?

Chapter 3

ANOTHER TICKING TAX BOMB

There is one more issue affecting your pension planning that we need to talk about before moving on: Alternative Minimum Tax, or AMT. If you haven't heard about it, don't worry—you will. It's not a new tax, but because of the way it was set up originally it is going to become a big tax.

Right now AMT is affecting about 4 million Americans. But the way the law stands right now (early 2006) about 20 million more Americans will start losing sleep over AMT in 2007. And the really lousy part is that most traditional tax planning is no match for AMT—in fact, AMT is going to screw up just about all tax planning. There are a couple of things you can do—but the secret is that you're going to have to be proactive to avoid the AMT trap.

ALTERNATIVE MINIMUM TAX—SO FAR, NO GOOD

Are you subject to AMT? You might be, if you are making more than $58,000 as a married couple filing jointly, $40,250 for a single taxpayer, or $29,000 for a married couple filing separately.*

How We Got Stuck with AMT

In 1969, the Treasury Department surveyed filed tax returns and found that a few hundred American taxpayers had avoided paying any tax at all through the clever use of legal, IRS-approved tax loopholes. These individuals were all considered wealthy at that time, earning $200,000 or more yearly (which would translate into about $1.4 million per year in today's dollars). The AMT was created in reaction to those few hundred taxpayers, as a way to make sure taxpayers could not loophole their way to a zero-dollar tax return.

But the income thresholds used to determine AMT liability weren't made using the same type of sliding scale we use for regular income tax calculations. Instead, these thresholds are rigid and are adjusted by Congress every few years. The last adjustment happened in late 2003, but it was only a temporary adjustment, and it expired at the end of 2005. That means the current AMT thresholds reverted to their 2001 levels, which are $49,000 for married couples filing jointly, $35,750 for single taxpayers, and $24,500 for married couples filing separately. What was meant to catch the very upper echelon of taxpayers has already ensnared an estimated 4 million American taxpayers for the 2005 tax year, and, by going back to the 2001 levels, a whopping 20 million Americans are expected to be caught in 2006, unless Congress intervenes and changes the thresholds.

---

*Find out if you're subject to AMT. We've got an AMT test you can take for free at www.reirallc.com.

Why It Won't Go Away

In case you're interested, about 2,700 taxpayers earning $1 million or more paid zero or little tax in 2003. Ironic, huh?

> AMT = the government's ATM

But, while AMT isn't doing what it was supposed to do, it *is* bringing in a lot of money for the government. And that's the problem. Our government, like most other governments, relies on the money we feed it each year to run smoothly. To really fix AMT— that is, to make sure the very wealthiest among us pay some tax— Congress would have to take a *huge* tax hit. Some economists and tax analysts estimate that up to 1 trillion dollars would need to be cut from expected tax income in the next 10 years to redesign AMT to do the job it was supposed to do. And, while governments like to issue tax breaks, they don't like them *that* much. So, even though it isn't doing the job it was supposed to, and even though there are still wealthy people paying little or no taxes, the middle class will continue to bear the AMT burden.

At this time (early 2006), there is legislation on the table to adjust the income thresholds for 2006 and 2007—in other words, Congress is slapping another Band-Aid on the problem.*

HOW IS AMT CALCULATED?

AMT is a flat-tax amount calculated at 26 percent on the first $175,000 of your income, and increases to 28 percent for income above that amount. This rate is not applied to your net income.

---

*Keep up to date on the latest tax law updates for AMT. Go to www.taxloopholes .com to register for free e-mail updates.

Instead, the AMT calculation begins with your adjusted gross income—that is, the income you had left over after taking off your standard or itemized deductions, but before your personal exemptions. Then the AMT forces you to add back in many of your standard or itemized deductions, which are now called "preference" items. What you wind up with is your AMTI (alternative minimum tax income). From there you can deduct the appropriate exemption amount, which scales back very quickly as your income rises. As your income exceeds $150,000 for married filing jointly ($112,500 for single and $75,000 for married filing separately) your AMTI exemption shrinks to almost nothing.

Preference Items

When loopholes aren't loopholes any longer. Some examples of preference items are:

- State taxes claimed as itemized deductions.
- Accelerated depreciation.
- Capital gains tax rates.

Under AMT rules, you lose all of these deductions.

If you've taken the free AMT test at www.reirallc.com and discovered it may affect you, you'll first need to calculate your taxes as you would regularly. Then you'll have to do them again, this time under the AMT method. Once you have the two sets prepared, compare the two, and be prepared to pay whichever one is higher.

WHO IS THE MOST IMPACTED BY AMT?

AMT actually impacts both personal and business taxpayers, but it is individuals who are bearing the heaviest burden. Loopholes

All of his friends thought Jack had it made. It was the year 2000, and he worked for Intuit with amazing stock options. He read in a leading financial publication that he should exercise those options because there wouldn't be any tax consequences. Jack was a real do-it-yourselfer when it came to taxes so he didn't consult any tax experts. Besides, he reasoned, this was a leading financial publication and they had just told millions of subscribers that this was the smart thing to do.

The problem was that Jack had never heard about AMT. The incentive stock options (ISOs) were subject to AMT calculation. So, although he didn't have income tax due, and in fact actually didn't have any cash in hand, he found out well into the next year that he owed a lot of tax. In fact, his tax rate ended up being 125 percent of his income. That's right—Jack owed more in taxes than he even made!

That was because he had exercised the stock options and now owned the stock. The problem was that Jack couldn't just sell the stock to pay the tax. (By the way, that's the reason that the leading financial publication had said to exercise. It would start the clock ticking for when the option holder did sell the stock. By exercising, he could get the much lower long-term capital gains tax rate. Otherwise, if he waited to exercise and then sell, he'd pay ordinary income tax rates.)

The reason that Jack couldn't just sell the stock is because the value had plummeted. If he sold and got a loss, which is what would happen, he'd only be able to write off a loss of $3,000 per year.

The moral of the story is to make sure you and your advisors take all possible consequences into account before you do any major transactions.

for businesses have kept coming over the years, to the point where most businesses no longer have to fear AMT. You and I, however, have not been given much to work with.

When taxpayers fall subject to AMT, they lose many of the deductions that were available before. It's especially bad if you live in a high-tax jurisdiction like California, New Hampshire, New York, Vermont, or Washington, D.C., because you lose the ability to deduct state income, sales, and property taxes. In fact, some studies estimate that 90 percent of taxpayers paying AMT now are paying it because they live in high-tax states.

So, just imagine the impact AMT is going to have on your pension. In Chapter 1, we laid out tables showing how much you'll need to save to create a yearly income of $60,000 or more. If you reach your goal, all of your hard work stands a very real chance of dropping you squarely into the AMT trap, and you can expect to pay more in taxes than you planned to. You finally pay off the mortgage, only to have increased taxes eat up that extra cash. But structuring your retirement plan to fall below the AMT income threshold isn't necessarily a good solution either. First, who knows where the threshold amounts will be when you retire, and, secondly, you stand a very real chance of not having enough to live on—or live on comfortably.

AMT KILLS TRADITIONAL TAX PLANNING

Unfortunately, the best income tax planning for regular taxes in the world won't help you if you fall into the AMT trap. In fact, it will probably hurt you, because many standard tax-planning strategies are completely backwards and counterproductive as far as AMT is concerned. You can even wind up paying more tax. And if you find out at the end of the year that you didn't meet the AMT threshold and don't have to pay it, then you'll wind up paying more, too. So the very first piece of planning you need to do is find out whether or not AMT is going to be a factor.

Determining if you will be subject to AMT should be the first part of your retirement tax strategy. Tax planning for AMT is different from tax planning for regular income tax.

After you've determined whether you might be subject to AMT, look up what AMT tax preference items will be applicable. Remember, the tax preference items are the items that will be added back to your taxable income to calculate your AMT income.

Avoiding AMT Altogether

Right now, some of you are probably thinking, "So, is that it? I'm going to be hit with this horrible tax and I should just get used to it? Thank you, Uncle Sam, may I please have another?" Well, don't despair. There are some things you can do with your regular tax planning to help avoid or minimize AMT.

As far as your pension and retirement planning is concerned, you have two excellent new choices that will both allow your pension income to come out the other end as not subject to AMT—no matter how much you're taking out. Again, though, you have to be proactive here. These are *not* choices that are going to be offered through your employer—in fact, in order to take advantage of these choices you're going to need your own business. Check out Chapter 6 to learn all about the Solo 401(k) and the Solo Roth 401(k)—the AMT busters.

SECTION TWO

Alternative Plans for Work and Retirement

Chapter 4

GETTING RICH IN TODAY'S WORLD

Today's world is expensive. Health care costs are high, housing is high, and a lot of folks work more than one job just to make ends meet. For many people, growing their wealth to provide enough for a comfortable retirement feels almost impossible. After the bills are paid and the kids are looked after, there's not much left over, and the thought of tying up all of that emergency cash in an inaccessible pension plan isn't very attractive.

We recognize that there are millions of Americans out there who would love to put more money towards their retirement, but don't feel they have the excess income to spare. And we also feel one of the things that most people who find themselves in this category have in common is the way they think about income. So in this chapter we'd like to introduce you to some ideas to help increase your income so you can begin to take advantage (or greater advantage) of the ideas presented elsewhere in this book.

UNDERSTANDING INCOME

How do you think about income? Is it strictly what you bring home from work? Or is your definition wider, leaving room for income from a hobby, a part-time business, from a stock portfolio or from rental real estate?

We believe that if you really want to create wealth in this world you're going to need more than just W-2 income. Here's a secret that really isn't: You're not going to get rich working for someone else. You can't make any more than your boss pays you, no matter how hard you work. Just as with employer-sponsored investing, you have a serious lack of control. To change that, you need to take control.

That doesn't necessarily mean you need to quit your job—you don't! But if you're serious about changing your current income level, to create the income you need now and for the future, then you do need to change how you may think about money, and more specifically, how you define (and make) income. There are actually three different types of income. Each of these forms of income is taxed differently.

EARNED INCOME

The IRS classifies income into three categories: earned, passive, and portfolio. Most people receive the bulk of their income as earned income. That's the income you take home on your W-2 or 1099. It's taxed at the highest rate—current federal rates are as high as 35 percent and that's before state tax rates are figured in—and it is subject to the fewest amount of deductions of any income type. So, you get to work hard and keep less.

However, simply by starting a small, part-time business, or turning a hobby into a business, you can begin to redefine your earned income. That's because this is income you control—you control how much you earn, how much time you devote to the hobby that creates the income, and so on. And, by operating a business even part-time, you have access to all of the tax deductions and loopholes that business owners receive. At the beginning, it's very likely that your business may have a loss—on paper at least—that you can then apply against your W-2 income. If you lower your W-2 income, your tax rate will lower as well—putting more money into your pocket at the end of the day.

PORTFOLIO INCOME

Portfolio income is the money you earn from stocks, bonds, mutual funds, as interest, dividends, or sales. If you receive a dividend on your stocks, or if you sell some mutual funds at a profit, you pay tax on the profit—but in most cases that tax will be lower than the tax on your W-2 or 1099 income. That's because dividends and long-term capital gains (capital gains that result from the sale of an asset that you have held for over a year), are taxed at a maximum of only 15 percent. Interest and short-term capital gains are taxed at the ordinary income tax rate.

PASSIVE INCOME

Although portfolio income sounds pretty good, we like passive income even more. Passive income is the best of all, because it has the potential to be tax-free.

Passive income is typically income you receive through real estate investments. It's passive because you don't personally do anything to earn it—it's coming from the rents your tenant pays you (or, more accurately, the business structure you set up to hold the real estate pays you its leftover profit after all expenses and deductions are taken out). And because there are so many tax deductions available on real estate investment property, including depreciation, the business structure that holds the real estate can actually show a paper loss on its books, which means it won't pay any tax—even though you probably received cash from that investment each and every month. At the same time that real estate property is appreciating in value, meaning that when you eventually sell the property you'll have another large chunk of cash that the IRS won't tax as earned income.

Consider this: if you leverage the equity in your home by getting a home equity loan or by refinancing your existing mortgage, you have a choice. You could use that equity to purchase a boat and, then you'd have a boat. Now use that same equity and buy a rental property. Charge enough rent to pay all of the mortgage, taxes, and other associated expenses. If you set up your investment structure correctly, there should be little or no tax payable on that property or the rental income you receive. After a few years, the property will have increased in value, even though you've put little or nothing into it. Can you say the same thing about your boat?

Good Assets:	Assets that put money in your pocket
Bad Assets:	Assets that take money out of your pocket

Which way does your cash flow?

How much of your income is earned, versus portfolio and passive? Here's a secret: if you were to look at the income streams of most wealthy people you'd see that earned income only makes up a small portion of their overall income. Something the wealthy understand very clearly is that the more you can replace earned income with portfolio and passive income, the lower your taxes will be.

CREATING WEALTH BEGINS AT HOME

Earlier, we mentioned the difference a home-based business can make to your taxes. Now, we'll take that one step further: if you want to grow your wealth in today's world, owning your own business is an essential part of your wealth-building strategy. The combination of additional income plus tax savings can add up to the money you need to start or grow your pension fund.

Diane first introduced the concept of "jump starting" your wealth in *Loopholes of the Rich* (John Wiley & Sons, 2005). What follows are some highlights of just how easy it can be to start creating wealth outside of your pension plan. If retirement is looming, and you're just starting to save, you're going to need all the help you can get to catch up. Jump Start may provide that help.

THE JUMP START PROGRAM

Jump Start works for taxpayers at all income levels. It's a seven-step program designed for people who want to change their lives by taking control and changing their wealth. These seven steps are the same for everyone, no matter where you are financially. That's because the critical element to Jump Start isn't how much money you make; it's how you make your money.

Here are the seven Jump Start steps:

Step 1: Create a business, and maximize your business income with tax loopholes.

Step 2: Maximize your tax-free benefits with tax loopholes by discovering your hidden business deductions.

Step 3: Once you have minimized your taxes from your business, pay your taxes.

Step 4: Invest in real estate, and maximize your real estate investments with real estate loopholes.

Step 5: Maximize your cash flow with real estate loopholes.

Step 6: Buy a house, and maximize your home investment with home loopholes.

Step 7: Get money out of your house! Maximize your cash flow with home loopholes.

CREATE A BUSINESS AND MAXIMIZE YOUR BUSINESS INCOME WITH TAX LOOPHOLES

Creating a business is Step 1. You must decide what type of business you will have, and from there, design your loophole strategy. This is where your wealth-building process really begins.

Businesses get the best tax breaks, which shouldn't come as a surprise. After all, businesses use supplies, offer services, manufacture products, and, most importantly, hire employees and advisors. People who work pay taxes and buy products. The more people who work, the stronger our economy.

The majority of tax loopholes are in areas that the government would like us to be more active—for example, in starting and operating your own businesses and investing in real estate. In fact, when it comes to having a home office, the IRS is downright aggressive in its promotion efforts.

MAXIMIZE YOUR TAX-FREE BENEFITS WITH TAX LOOPHOLES BY DISCOVERING YOUR HIDDEN BUSINESS DEDUCTIONS

In Step 2, you discover your "hidden" business deductions. These are expenses that you currently pay with after-tax money. Now, with a legitimate business (don't forget Step 1!), you can look at these expenses with new eyes. In this step, we review the theory behind what is deductible, look at more than 300 items that could be expensed, and then work through an exercise to review every single personal expense that you have.*

Remember, though, that you must have a legitimate business and a legitimate business purpose for the expenses you deduct. The IRS takes a very dim view of the periodic hustlers who sell people on the idea that they can set up a nonexistent business just to write off personal expenses. You must have a business purpose, and you must have a real business.

ONCE YOU HAVE MINIMIZED YOUR TAXES FROM YOUR BUSINESS, PAY YOUR TAXES

Step 3 is to pay your taxes. No, that's not a misprint. There's a big difference between evading taxes (which is illegal) and avoiding taxes (reducing your taxes through legal methods).

Steps 1 and 2 helped you reduce the amount of taxes you will pay through legal means. Step 3 of Jump Start, takes a look at the way you currently pay taxes and shows you different ways to pay your taxes that can benefit you. This step can even work for your W-2 income! But it works even better if you're also a business owner.

---

*Visit www.realestateirallc.com to download a copy of the 300+ deductions you can use in your business.

INVEST IN REAL ESTATE, AND MAXIMIZE YOUR REAL ESTATE INVESTMENTS WITH REAL ESTATE LOOPHOLES

The first three Jump Start steps dealt with starting a business and taking advantage of all of the deductions and loopholes available to business owners. Steps 4 through 7 all relate to real estate. Why? Because real estate grows wealth quickly, especially when you take advantage of the Jump Start leverage and velocity wealth-building strategies.

In Step 4, you get started buying real estate. We show you how to look for good, solid real estate investments that will return positive cash flow to you. The goal is to invest as much as possible from your business income into real estate. In fact, your ultimate goal will be to receive mainly passive income. In Step 3 you learned about the types of taxable income and their tax rates. Passive income has the lowest rate of taxable income, so you can use the money from your business to build a basis of real estate for yourself.

MAXIMIZE YOUR CASH FLOW WITH REAL ESTATE LOOPHOLES

As your property appreciates in value, what you do with that money becomes important. That's where Step 5 comes in. We show you how to leverage the equity in your properties to build your portfolio quickly and with minimum risk.

BUY A HOUSE, AND MAXIMIZE YOUR HOME INVESTMENT WITH HOME LOOPHOLES

In Step 6, it's time to buy your home. And while creating a business first and buying a home second may seem backward, if you think about it for a few minutes it makes sense. By creating a business first and investing its profits into real estate investments, you have created sources of income for yourself that can help you to buy the home you want—and in the most tax-advantaged way. Your equity and assets will help you secure a good mortgage on terms beneficial to you. That means you can buy the smart way—making sure that you don't overextend yourself financially. And, finally, you can make sure you have asset protection on your home by using a protected business structure, like a limited liability company, to hold the title instead of holding it personally.

GET MONEY OUT OF YOUR HOUSE! MAXIMIZE YOUR CASH FLOW WITH HOME LOOPHOLES

In Step 6, you bought your home. In Step 7, it's time to ask yourself this: How can you turn your house purchase from a liability (something that takes money from your pocket) into an asset (something that puts money into your pocket)? In Step 7, you will discover some of the home loopholes available for the innovative home owner, including the two-out-of-five-year rule. This rule says that once you have lived in your home for at least two years out of the preceding five years, you can sell the property and take the first $250,000 in gain tax-free (or $500,000, if you're a married couple who file a joint tax return).

Diane has clients that do nothing more than take advantage of one or more of these home loopholes to increase their wealth. One of Diane's clients takes advantage of the two-out-of-five-year rule to live in homes that he rehabilitates. He always chooses older neighborhoods that are on their way up. He buys a house, fixes it up, and then sells it—collecting his profit tax-free!

Of course, pulling off a plan like that needs good financing, credit lines, or a cash reserve to get you started and through the first couple of years. After that, you can often coast on the money you received from the sale of the prior property. The point is, your home can be an asset if you are prepared to look at home ownership just a little bit differently from how you may have done in the past.

JUMP-START HELPS YOU TAKE CONTROL

As we said at the beginning of this chapter, the more control you have over how you make money, the more money you can make. If you're wondering how to create the money to fund your pension plan, Jump Start ideas can help you get there.

If you use your home-based business profits to invest in rental real estate (or the excess cash you generate through paying less tax), you accomplish two things: first, you create another source of income for yourself. Even if your properties are barely cash-flow positive, as long as you have a few more dollars coming in than going out at the end of the day, you have created another income source. Second, you create another powerful source of deductions. The depreciation and other expenses that come with rental real estate can create paper losses, and all of those paper losses can flow back against your income, reducing, or maybe even eliminating, your tax bill entirely.

Perhaps the most important element of rental real estate, though, is the appreciation that these properties are going to experience over time. You can leverage that appreciation by refinancing, pulling equity out, and reinvesting that equity in additional properties. You can thus create a self-sustaining income portfolio that is going to continue to grow over time.

Make no mistake about it. There is a finite supply of real estate in the United States and an increasing population. Everyone needs to live somewhere. Real estate is a potent source of income, wealth, and financial security for millions of people around the world. Your home-based business can help you get there.

APPLYING JUMP START PRINCIPLES
TO YOUR PENSION

The same reasons that make real estate such a powerful tool in your day-to-day income life can also apply to your pension activities. Imagine using a home-based business to create income, and putting that income into a self-directed pension plan. In fact, imagine putting that income into a tax-later or tax-never pension plan. Now imagine using that pension plan to purchase appreciating rental real estate instead of slow-moving stock. This time, when you sell the property or refinance down the road, all the money you are creating is also either tax-deferred or tax-free. Remember, the two-out-of- five-year rule only works for the home you are personally living in. But by using a tax-deferred or tax-free pension plan to purchase real estate, all of the homes you purchase with those pension funds will create tax-deferred or tax-free money through appreciation and resale.

Chapter 5

SAVING FOR RETIREMENT

B ack in Chapter 1, we made a statement that we disliked traditional retirement planning because it only worked if you were planning to be poor—in other words, when you retired you planned to downgrade your lifestyle and live on less than you currently have. That's because traditional retirement planning uses mostly deferred-tax pension plans, and not tax-free pension plans. Deferred-tax planning is, we think, the biggest gotcha in the pension industry. That's because people start to think that tax later somehow becomes tax never.

In the tax world, there is a saying that you never want to have the tax tail wagging the economic dog. In other words, tax considerations have to take a backseat to the more important goal, which is saving enough for your retirement. It may well be that investing with your tax-deferred plan is the best thing you can do for your retirement goals. Remember, your first priority should be building for retirement—any way you can—and if that's where your money is right now, so be it. After you make sure you're protected, then you can consider whether there is a more tax-advantaged way to move forward.

With that said, let's explore deferred-tax and tax free investing. Let's first go through the difference between deferred-tax and tax-free plans. Then we'll take a look at your retirement plan options.

DEFERRED-TAX PLANS: TAXING THE CROP

There's another saying that fits here. It says, "Tax the crop, not the seeds." By providing you with a tax break up front the IRS has ensured that it will have a fine crop to tax.

A tax-deferred plan is one where you put off paying the tax until later. This is the one you're probably most familiar with: your 401(k), SEP-IRA or regular IRA. Your employer withholds your contributions from your salary or, if you're self-employed or operate your own business, you make your own contributions.

Tax-deferred plans are the ones that everyone likes at tax time, because you get to take a tax deduction for all of the money you put in each year.

But even though that sounds great, there is a downside: you have to pay tax later, when the money comes out. That means the *only* way you can save any taxes using this method is if you plan to make less when you retire than you do while you're building your pension. This plan is presented to you with ribbons and bows as though it's the greatest thing since sliced bread, and millions of Americans buy into it every year—and the ultimate beneficiary isn't you at all—it's the IRS!

Here's why. When you take money out of your pension plan, that money is taxed at your ordinary, earned income tax rate—in other words, if you take out $60,000 from your 401(k) each year, you'll pay the exact same federal income tax as if you had a W-2 from your employer showing you were paid a $60,000 salary. Depending on how much you are drawing from your pension each year, you could wind up in a higher tax bracket—maybe even the top bracket of 35 percent. Or you could wind up in the AMT trap. And this assumes the IRS makes no changes to our current tax brackets between now and the time you retire—which is pretty unlikely. With this tax plan, the only way you can lower your tax rate would be to take out less each year—and lower your standard of living accordingly.

There's something else you need to think about here. When you're beginning your working life, you're probably going to be making less than you will be at the other end of your working life. Over the years, you will have grown and expanded your skill set to become a much more valuable employee, or you may have taken those skills and created your own business. Regardless, with few exceptions, your salary at the beginning of your working life probably isn't going to be anywhere close to that of the president of the company you work for. And even if you're starting your own business as an entrepreneur, chances are you won't reach your full earnings potential for a few years or more. Now during this time, you won't be paying as much in tax, right? The lower your income, the lower the taxes you'll pay. So what happens when you begin taking that money out after retirement? You are almost *assured* of paying more tax to take that money out than you would have paid when you were younger. In fact, you would probably have been better served to have paid the tax due at the time and invested that money somewhere else instead.

We think there's a better way. Use a tax-free retirement plan and tax the seeds instead.

Two Ways That Tax-Deferred Plans Can Get You

1. If your tax bracket is low now but will be higher later, you've traded low tax for high tax.
2. If the income you're deferring is considered long-term capital gains (from the sale of assets held over a year), you've traded capital gains income (maximum 15 percent tax rate) for ordinary income (maximum 35 percent tax rate).

TAX-FREE PLANS: TAXING THE SEEDS

If you had a choice between tax later or tax never, which would you choose? (We bet you say, "tax never.")

If you use a tax-free plan instead of a tax-deferred plan, you pay tax the other way—at the time you contribute money to your plan. So, you lose the tax deduction you get with a tax-deferred plan. But—and this is an important "but"—here's the trade-off: with a tax-free plan, all of the interest and growth your tax-free plan receives over the years comes out tax-free when you retire and begin making withdrawals.

Consider this: you contributed $100,000 after-tax dollars into a tax-free plan, where time and appreciation worked together to grow that plan to $1 million by the time you retire. All of that money is tax-free when it comes out. No federal tax, no AMT, nothing. Contrast that with contributing $100,000 in before-tax dollars into a tax-deferred plan. You would have received a tax break on the $100,000 of, say, 35 percent (assuming you were in the highest tax bracket). So you saved $35,000 in taxes by plowing that money into a tax-deferred plan. But 35 percent of $1 million is $350,000—which is the tax you're going to now pay to take that money out of your pension. That's not our idea of a good trade-off, and it's why we don't recommend that your retirement options consist exclusively of a tax-deferred plan.

IS THERE ROOM FOR BOTH?

Some of you might be asking why you'd want to do both, if tax-free plans are such a good deal. Well, the downside to tax-free plans is that in many cases the amount you can contribute is defined by your income level. And although there aren't any income limitations on the new solo Roth 401(k) plans, it also has a contribution limit.*

Here's something else to consider: If you work for an employer who offers a full or partial matching policy for the company 401(k) plan, then you're literally leaving money on the table if you don't contribute enough to make sure you get your employer's full matching funds. Free money is free money in this case. Yes, you'll have to pay tax on it when you withdraw those funds, but the more funds that go into your pension plan, the faster it will grow, and the extra value you'll receive at the other end will offset the taxes. And you'll also have the benefit of paying lower taxes now, while you're contributing to the tax-deferred plan—which means you could take the tax money you save and contribute that to a tax-free plan. Talk about having your money work for you!

YOUR RETIREMENT PLAN OPTIONS

There is a staggering amount of retirement plan types out there. Some you're probably quite familiar with, while others may be new, or simply terms you've seen without really understanding what they are.

As a rule you can divide plans into two categories: tax-deferred and tax-free. From there, you can subdivide them into employer-administered plans and personal, self-directed plans. We've set

---

*Tax law is constantly changing. For the latest contribution and income limitations, please visit Diane's web site at www.taxloopholes.com.

To Tax Defer or Not to Tax Defer?

Jason, Age 25

Jason's head was spinning from all of the options. He was 25 years old and discovered he could contribute up to $5,000 into his 401(k) each year. He was currently at a 35 percent tax rate and figured his investments would grow at 10 percent per year. He knew that the gains he'd make on the pension would be capital gains, if he did it with after-tax money. That meant the income would have been taxed at a maximum of 15 percent. If he puts the money into his pension plan and makes exactly the same investments, it'll be taxed at his ordinary income tax rate when he takes the money out. That could mean 35 percent or more. So, does it make sense to do a tax-deferred plan if it means he'll pay a higher rate later. And the administrator needs to know what he plans to do with his possible 401 (k) plan right now. Jason's question is, "Should I invest in a tax-deferred account?"

After Tax Plan: He'd just take the $5,000 per year in after-tax money. He wouldn't contribute to the 401(k) and instead pay tax on the income. He'd invest what is left into the proposed investments ($3,250) at 10 percent. He'd then pay long-term capital gains tax of 15 percent tax rate on the income.

Tax Deferred Plan: He'd take the $5,000 (all of it, because there is no tax) and then invest it at 10 percent. However, he'd pay 35 percent when he took the money out at the end.

What's the best answer? Do the math!

After Tax Plan:	$967,622
Tax Deferred Plan:	$1,451,798

Scott, Age 60

Jason's co-worker, Scott, was faced with the same dilemma. Should he contribute to the tax-deferred plan or not? Everything was the same, except that Scott was 60 years old, planning to retire in 5 years.

What's the best plan for Scott? Do the math!

Tax Deferred Plan: $20,317
After Tax Plan $19,640

The longer you have until retirement, the more advantageous the tax-deferred plan becomes. Of course, tax free is still better than either choice!*

---

*Would you like to discover what the best plan is for you, based on your personal circumstances? Come to www.reirallc.com to see whether the tax deferred or tax free plan will work for you. It's free and it's available to you as a special service as a reader of *The Insider's Guide to Tax-Free Real Estate Investing*.

out a chart below giving you a quick run-through of the most popular plans. There are more tax-deferred plan types than any others because these have been around the longest.

Tax-Deferred Plans	Tax-Free Plans	New Kids in Town
Traditional 401(k)[a]	Roth IRA[b]	Solo 401(k)[c]
Traditional IRA[b]	Education[b]	Solo Roth 401(k)[c]
Rollover IRA[b]	(Coverdell) IRA	
SEP IRA[a]		
SIMPLE IRA[a]		
Charitable IRA[b]		
Spousal IRA[b]		
Beneficiary IRAs[b]		
Conduit IRA[b]		

---

[a]Employer-administered plans.
[b]Personal, self-directed plans.
[c]Combine both employer-administered and self-directed qualities. These are discussed in detail in Chapter 6.

SELF-DIRECTED PLANS

There's nothing official about self-directed plans. In fact, you won't even find the term *self-directed* in the IRS Code. It's not a different type of IRA or 401(k) plan. It simply means that the owner of the plan (usually an IRA or a Solo 401(k), either regular or Roth) has greater control over their investment decisions, and not everything is left to the trustee or administrator.

As we've said, the level of control varies depending on the plan. You will probably find an employer-sponsored plan to be the most limited, and a self-directed Roth IRA or Solo Roth 401(k) pretty much limitless (within reason). That doesn't mean anything goes, however. You still do have to follow some rules on investments. But, it's a pretty simple list. We'll discuss more about self-directed plans in Chapter 7.

Traditional 401(k)

The 401(k) plan is the most familiar plan for most Americans. It's the one most commonly offered by employers. You can even set up a 401(k) if you're a sole proprietor or a self-employed person earning 1099 income.

A traditional 401(k) is the most common of the defined-contribution plans. It is governed by Section 401(k) of the Internal Revenue Code (hence the catchy name) and is a tax-deferred plan where you are allowed to set aside a certain portion of your yearly salary ($15,000 in 2006, although if you are 50 or older you can contribute up to $20,000 in 2006). That money is not taxed. It will appear on your W-2 as part of your overall salary, but you will also receive a tax credit equal to that amount on your return—which means that your income will be lowered before any tax is calculated. Depending on your current salary and the amount you put into your 401(k), you could find yourself dropping right out of your current tax bracket to a bracket one or two steps lower.

That's nice, because now all of your remaining income will be taxed at that lower rate.

Sometimes, you get lucky and work for an employer who matches your contributions with a contribution of their own. It could be the same amount or it could be a lower percentage of your contributions. If this happens, great! Your employer's contributions don't count against your contribution maximum, nor do they count against your salary. And sometimes you get really lucky and find yourself working for an employer who makes contributions for you, regardless of whether or not you make contributions yourself (but there aren't too many of these employers out there).

A 401(k) plan has some other advantages, too. For example, if you leave your job and go somewhere else, you can take your 401(k) plan with you. This is called "rolling over" and means that you transfer your existing funds to your new employer's 401(k) plan or even to an IRA. There is no tax consequence to doing this unless you move your funds from a tax-deferred plan to a tax-free plan. And, under federal law, 401(k) plans are protected from creditors in the case of personal bankruptcy. The Employment Retirement Income Security Act (or ERISA) protects 401(k) plans and some other types of retirement accounts from being seized and liquidated by creditors. That is, most creditors—ERISA won't protect your 401(k) plan from being seized to pay off a divorce order or a qualified child support order.

But, as we've already said, there are disadvantages to a 401(k) plan, too. The biggest one is taxation—the tax credit at the beginning is great, but it is completely overshadowed by the amount of tax you will pay at the other end when you begin making withdrawals from your 401(k). Here are some other disadvantages.

- As this is supposed to be a retirement account it's hard to get your money out before you turn $59^1/_2$. The IRS does have a list of contingencies for withdrawal (health or education expenses, and, most recently, to help those affected by Hurricanes Katrina, Rita and Wilma), but even if you are allowed to take out money, it will be taxed and may also be penalized for early withdrawal.

- Although you can begin taking withdrawals after you reach age 59^1/$_2$, you don't have to—you can leave that money in there to continue growing. But on April 1 of the year you turn 70^1/$_2$, those withdrawals (and the resulting tax payments) become mandatory.

- There may be strings attached to employer contributions. Most commonly, this means you must continue working for your employer for a set period of time before your contributions "vest," or come under your total control. If you go to work for someone else before the vesting period is over you may lose all or a portion of your employer's contributions. But your employer can't make the vesting conditions too onerous. By law, if your employer requires a vesting period before you receive total control over their contributions, your employer must either vest all of their contributions by your third year of employment, or vest 20 percent portions in Years 2 through 6 of your employment.

- Be wary of employers who only offer matching contributions if you use your 401(k) funds to invest in their stock. This is the trap that many people fell into with the recent accounting scandals. Enron, for example, only offered 100 percent contribution matches where all of the employee's contributions went into purchasing Enron stock. So when Enron went under and its stock fell to just pennies on the dollar, the value of these 401(k) plans fell, too.

- If you and your spouse (if you are married) don't use up all of your 401(k) funds during your lifetimes, the remaining funds become subject to federal and state income and estate taxes. Depending on where you live those taxes can take half, to three-quarters, or even more of your 401(k) funds before that money passes on to your heirs.

The money can be invested in a variety of ways within the plan itself, and the investments are largely self-directed—meaning that you can control how your money is invested. But as we've said, your investment options are limited to those that are offered by the 401(k). Typically you can expect to find the opportunity to invest in your employer's stock, certain mutual funds, and U.S. Savings Bonds. The only way to move outside of these choices is to change jobs—you don't have the ability to truly self-direct your retirement funds in this instance.

Traditional IRA

The traditional deductible IRA was created for individuals that don't participate in an employer-sponsored retirement plan, although sometimes you can still qualify for this type of plan even if you do contribute to a 401(k). It works in much the same way as a 401(k), in that you deduct your contributions from your annual income before it is taxed, and you pay tax when you take the money back out. But whether you can deduct the entire amount you put into your traditional IRA depends on several things, including your tax-filing status (married filing jointly or married filing separately), whether or not you or your spouse participate in a 401(k) through your employer, and how much your adjusted gross income is.

Your maximum yearly contribution into a traditional IRA is $4,000 in 2006. If you're married, each spouse can contribute $4,000, for a maximum of $8,000 per year, per couple. This amount is set to rise in 2008 to $5,000 per year, per person and in 2009 some additional cost of living allowances are set to kick in after that which will increase the contribution limit by $500 per year, per person. Once you turn 50 you also become eligible to contribute catch up amounts of $1,000 per year, per person.

The deadline for making an IRA contribution is usually April 15 of the following year (meaning for the 2006 tax year you can make contributions up to April 15, 2007, and so on). However, once you turn $70^{1}/_{2}$ you cannot make any more IRA contributions.

You can begin tapping into your traditional IRA at age $59^{1}/_{2}$, either as a lump sum or in partial withdrawals. Just like a 401(k) though, once you turn $70^{1}/_{2}$ deductions become mandatory. The amount of tax you will pay depends on how much money you make in each year you withdraw funds. So from a tax perspective it may be good to lower your income as much as possible in a year you know you will have to take an IRA distribution.

A traditional IRA has other things in common with a 401(k) plan as well. For example;

- An ex-spouse can seize an IRA to make good a divorce order or a child support proceeding. If this happens and you are younger than $59^{1}/_{2}$, however, the IRS will give you a break on the penalty for early withdrawal.
- The same estate taxes that apply to your 401(k) apply to your traditional IRA as well. So as part of your estate planning you may want to cash out your traditional IRA at some point and put the money into a tax-free retirement plan, to avoid huge estate taxes.

One advantage a traditional IRA enjoys over a 401(k) is a wider range of investment options. That's because, unlike a 401(k), you can set up your traditional IRA to be truly self-directed. Now, in addition to the basics—stocks, bonds, mutual funds, annuities, certificates of deposit—you can tell your IRA custodian (the person or company who, in essence, manages your IRA) what you want to invest the money in—be it real estate, bare land, REITs, and more.

Rollover (Noncontributory) IRA

This type of IRA was designed as a holding account for funds distributed from a qualified retirement plan such as 401(k) and

403(b). Prior to 2002, there were some benefits to maintaining a separate IRA just for the rollovers from these types of accounts. After 2002, it was no longer as necessary to maintain rollover IRAs because a traditional IRA provided the same benefits.

SEP IRA

A SEP (Simplified Employee Pension) IRA is an employee benefit plan with compliance and reporting requirements that are simpler than those for qualified plans such as 401(k) and 403(b) plans. For this reason, SEP IRAs are often used by small companies who don't have the time or resources to administer a full 401(k) or 403(b) plan. Any employer can offer a SEP IRA—even if you are a sole proprietor.

Contributions to a SEP are limited to 25 percent of adjusted gross income or $44,000 (for 2006), whichever is less. The maximum compensation (defined as earned income) upon which SEP contributions can be based is $220,000. As a tax-deferred retirement plan, every dollar contributed to a SEP IRA is deductible.

SEP participants can also contribute up to $4,000 (or $4,500 in 2005, if over 50) to a SEP IRA. However, because a SEP is an employee benefit retirement plan, an active participant in a SEP may not be able to deduct non-SEP contributions. For this reason, it might make more sense to explore making IRA contributions by the employee directly into a traditional IRA.

SIMPLE IRA

The SIMPLE IRA (Savings Incentive Match Plan for Employees) is another plan designed for small businesses—in this case those with 100 or fewer employees. With a SIMPLE IRA employees can contribute up to $10,000 per year for 2006 if you are under age 50, and $12,500 if you are age 50 and over. These amounts are set to be indexed for inflation beginning in 2007, meaning they will rise each year. Because a SIMPLE IRA is a match plan, your employer is required to make a contribution as well—currently up to 3 percent of whatever you contribute.

All contributions to a SIMPLE IRA are fully deductible by both the employee and the employer. For employees the tax is deferred until the money is withdrawn, just as with all tax-deferred plans. However, if you withdraw money from your SIMPLE IRA within the first two years of participating in that plan, you cannot roll that money over into a Roth IRA or into any other type of IRA, other than another SIMPLE IRA.

Charitable IRA

A charitable IRA is a self-directed IRA that is sponsored or promoted by a nonprofit or charitable institution. It's generally a traditional IRA, subject to regular IRA rules, with a third-party administrator who supports this type of plan.

The charity or nonprofit establishes an IRA investment vehicle to help fund a charitable goal. The investment vehicle may be in any of a number of different forms, such as a bond or loan, which pays a fixed interest rate, or an equity interest in a limited liability company, a limited partnership, or corporate entity. The charity will set the investment terms and conditions, such as the duration or minimum investment amount.

The charity receives income from the IRA investments in one or more of the following ways:

- An annual distribution based on income in the IRA account.
- Minimum predetermined distributions from the IRA to fund tax deductible contributions.
- As beneficiary of the IRA upon death of the principal.

You can designate a charity or a group of charities as the beneficiary of your Charitable IRA. During your lifetime, you receive the benefit of the IRA. You need to follow the standard rules and contribution limits, and you must start taking withdrawals at age 70$^1/_2$. The amount that is withdrawn is taxed to the recipient at their income tax rate. A 1099R will be provided to them annually reflecting the amount of the withdrawal. When you pass away, the balance of your IRA will be transferred to the charity or charities you listed.

Spousal IRA

A spousal IRA enables an earning spouse to fund an IRA for the other spouse, who is not currently earning. In this way, a couple could contribute up to $8,000 or more if one or both are age 50.

There are a few rules for a spousal IRA:

- The couple must be married.
- At least one spouse must have compensation.
- The couple must file a federal tax return as married, filing jointly.
- An IRA must be established for the non-compensated spouse.
- The noncompensated spouse must be under the age of 70$^1/_2$.

Each spouse must have separate IRAs. In other words, both spouses cannot contribute to the same IRA. If the noncompensated spouse later receives compensation, he or she can contribute to the spousal IRA, however. It is not necessary to open up an additional IRA.

Beneficiary IRAs

If you inherit an IRA, you are called a beneficiary. A beneficiary can be any person or entity the owner chooses to receive the benefits of the IRA upon death. There are some further distinctions of beneficiary IRAs.

Spousal Inheritance IRA. If you inherit a traditional IRA from your spouse, you generally have the following three choices. You can:

1. Treat it as your own IRA by designating yourself as the account owner.
2. Treat it as your own by rolling it over into your traditional IRA.
3. Treat yourself as the beneficiary rather than treating the IRA as your own.

Inherited IRA. If you inherit an IRA from anyone other than your deceased spouse, you cannot treat the inherited IRA as your own. This means that you cannot make any contributions to the IRA. It also means you cannot roll over any amounts into or out of the inherited IRA.

Like the original owner, you generally will not owe tax on the assets in the IRA until you receive distributions from it.

Conduit IRA

A conduit IRA is an IRA that is funded solely from amounts attributable to a rollover from a qualified retirement plan, tax-sheltered annuity (403(b)) plan, or governmental eligible deferred compensation (457(b)) plan and earnings on those amounts.

Recent changes to the tax laws permit plans to accept rollovers from IRAs funded with any type of before-tax contributions. However, many plans choose to accept rollovers from an IRA only if the IRA is funded exclusively with amounts rolled in from one of the plans mentioned above. For that reason, conduit IRAs are useful because they preserve an IRA owner's option to roll back funds into a plan that limits rollovers from IRAs.

Roth IRA

The highly popular Roth IRA (named for the senator from Delaware who introduced the idea to Congress) has been around since 1997. It's really a simple process—in fact, there are just three steps.

1. Open a Roth IRA account with a qualified plan administrator (you'll find a list of companies we've found particularly helpful on our web site, www.reirallc.com).
2. Contribute to your Roth IRA using after-tax dollars in the same way you would a basic savings account and watch it grow over time.
3. Take the money out, tax-free (if you take the money out within five years of putting it in, though, you will pay a 10 percent penalty).

Now before you pull out your checkbook, there are a few limitations. First is a contribution limitation. You can only contribute $4,000 per year, per person ($5,000 per year, per person, if you're over 50). These limits are set to rise in 2008 to $5,000 and $6,000, respectively. You can't contribute $4,000 to a regular IRA and then $4,000 to a Roth IRA, either. All IRA contributions are aggregated when it comes to applying the contribution limit.

Second, as your income rises your contribution limit decreases. As your income tops $95,000 for a single person or $150,000 for a married couple filing jointly, your contribution limit goes down. By the time you reach $110,000 for a single ($160,000 for married, filing jointly), you are barred from contributing to a Roth IRA at all. And if you are married but file a separate return one year, you won't be able to make a Roth IRA contribution during that tax year.

There is a phase-out period for income between $150,000 and $160,000 for married and between $95,000 and $110,000 for single. A married taxpayer filing a separate return for a year generally may not contribute to a Roth IRA for that year.

Because you are putting the money in with after-tax dollars, you can withdraw it at any time after you reach age $59\frac{1}{2}$, although there is a penalty if you've had your Roth IRA open for five years or less. Sometimes, you can get around this, if you make what's called a "qualified" distribution. These are exceptions that the IRS has made to this rule, including withdrawals made for medical expenses, if you become permanently disabled, education expenses, and for first-time home purchases, But there is no mandatory distribution requirement when you reach age $70\frac{1}{2}$. There's no contribution limit, either. You can contribute to your Roth IRA right up until the day you die.

Education (Coverdell) IRA

A Coverdell IRA (also called an Education Savings Account, or an ESA) is a special account set up to pay for the qualified education expenses of a designated beneficiary. Unless your beneficiary is considered a special needs student, he or she must be under age 18 when you set up your ESA.

If you are familiar with the characteristics and functions of a Roth IRA, you now understand the Coverdell ESA, as they offer similar benefits. Contributions into a Coverdell IRA are not tax-deductible, and are made with after-tax dollars. You can take the money out tax-free in the future although it can be taxed if the money isn't used to pay qualified education expenses. You can contribute a maximum of $2,000 each year for each beneficiary, using one or more ESAs, as long as your income is less than $110,000 ($220,000 for couples who are married, filing jointly).

You must have distributed the entire ESA by the time your student beneficiary turns 30, unless he or she is a special needs student. And if your designated beneficiary stops attending school, you can switch beneficiaries to another student, as long as that person is under the age of 30.

Some other points to note on ESAs include the following:

- Your beneficiary can withdraw the money tax-free in any year that he or she incurs qualified education expenses.
- Expenses may include tuition, fees, academic tutoring, special needs services, books, supplies, and other equipment, which are incurred in connection to your beneficiary's enrollment at an eligible educational institution.
- In 2002, the meaning of "qualified education expenses" was expanded to include both elementary and secondary education.
- Allowable expenses for K–12 also include room and board, uniforms, transportation, and supplementary items and services (including extended day programs), as well as computer technology or equipment.
- If your beneficiary withdraws more than is needed for the qualified higher education expense, the earnings portion of the excess withdrawal is subject to income tax and, in some circumstances, a 10 percent penalty.

One other thing to be aware of here is that the amount of qualified education expenses will be reduced by any other tax-free benefits received in that year. In essence, the IRS will not allow your child to "double-dip" into multiple tax-free benefit plans for overlapping expenses.

WHAT TO DO IF YOU'RE STUCK
IN THE WRONG PLAN

If after reading this chapter you've decided you want to change plans, the good news is—you can—and often without paying any tax or penalties! For example, a traditional IRA can be rolled over or converted penalty-free to a Roth IRA, as long as your AGI (Adjusted Gross Income) (or your joint AGI if you're married, filing jointly) is not more than $100,000 in the year you do the rollover. If you're married, you must file a joint return to qualify here—married, filing separately couples cannot take advantage of this option. For the purposes of determining whether you have reached the $100,000 limit, your AGI is determined before any amount is included in your income as a result of the rollover.* Of course, you will have to pay tax on the converted amount.

There are some rules related to the rollover. For example, any rollover must be a qualified rollover contribution. The rollover contribution must be completely rolled into the qualified Roth plan within a 60-day time limit rule.

As long as you have a qualified plan administrator involved in the process and you follow their instructions, you shouldn't have any problems moving your money. We talk more about rolling over and how to move your money effectively from one plan to another in Chapter 17.

---

*A recent tax law change will allow all taxpayers, regardless of income, the ability to roll a traditional IRA into a Roth IRA. This is a one-year-only opportunity, though, effective only in 2010. For more on new tax law changes in this area, go to www.reiralllc.com.

THE NEW KIDS IN TOWN: SOLO 401(K)
AND SOLO ROTH 401(K) PLANS

In the next chapter, we'll be taking a look at two of the most excit-
ing developments in pension planning and investing since the
Roth IRA. The Solo 401(k) began in January 2002, while the Solo
Roth 401(k) plan came into effect in January 2006. Between them,
these two plans could offer everything you ever needed in your
retirement plan. We believe that as their benefits become more
widely known the impact of these two plans on American retirement savings will be huge.

Chapter 6

NEW STRATEGIES FOR NEW PLANS

B ack in Chapter 4 we talked about the difficulties in saving for retirement in today's world, and why starting a home-based business, even a small, part-time one, can help, through a combination of additional income and reduced taxes. But if you need another reason to consider starting a business—or two reasons—then this is the chapter for you. That's because the two pension plans presented in this chapter are only available to people with their own businesses.

There are three basic rules for these types of plans:

1. You and your spouse are the only full-time employees allowed.
2. You have to draw a salary from the business.
3. You have to contribute the right kind of income.

Let's explore this third requirement in a little more detail.

THERE ARE THREE WAYS TO EARN INCOME—
BUT ONLY TWO WILL WORK!

There are three different ways you can make money through a business structure. First, you can operate as an independent contractor, through what's called a Sole Proprietorship. If you work alone, and don't have a formal business structure, the government defaults you to this structure for tax purposes. In this type of business structure you'll receive 1099 income from people and businesses you do work for. That's fine—you can use 1099 income to fund either of the plans in this chapter.

The second way you can make money is to receive a salary through a formal business structure. An S Corporation or a C Corporation are both examples of this. If you operate through either of these business structures, you'll receive W-2 income, and that's also fine, as W-2 income is acceptable for either of these two plans. (Actually, both of these business types also allow you to take some money out as profit-sharing, but that portion will be treated a bit differently when you put it into one of these plans.)

If you own multiple companies, beware of controlled group issues (that's where you own a majority interest in one or more C Corporations). Companies that form part of a controlled group are prohibited from setting up a Solo 401(k) plan—any plan they set up will automatically become a traditional 401(k) plan instead.

The third way you can make money is to receive profit-sharing distributions only. The money you receive as a member of a limited liability company (LLC) or a limited partnership (LP) are examples of this type of income. This income comes out of the business to you on a Schedule K-1, and that means it won't work for these types of plans. You've got to have some 1099 or W-2 income first.

EXPLORING THE SOLO 401(K)

The Solo 401(k) is not an IRA, but in many ways it acts like one because you can self-direct the plan. This new plan was created in October 2001, but came into force in January of 2002. The Solo 401(k) plan is like a traditional 401(k) plan in some ways. It needs an employer to oversee it. The money contributed is tax-deferred, so you receive a deduction on your income tax return and pay taxes when the money is withdrawn. There is no upper income limit to contribute to a Solo 401(k) plan—you can make as much as you want. You can begin taking distributions at age $59\frac{1}{2}$, and after you hit $70\frac{1}{2}$ those distributions become mandatory. After that, though, things begin to change as the IRA characteristics kick in.

First of all, a Solo 401(k) is available to anyone with a business—incorporated or not, as long as you (and your spouse, if you have one) are the only full-time employees, and you receive either 1099 or W-2 income. If you have part-time employees, they must work no more than 1,000 hours per year, per employee. Otherwise, your Solo 401(k) plan will be converted by the IRS into a standard 401(k) plan, and all of the traditional rules will apply instead.

The next major difference is in contribution limits. A traditional 401(k) limits your yearly contributions to $15,000 in 2006 ($20,000 if you're over 50), and because this is an employer-sponsored plan, those contributions must come from your salary earnings. A Solo 401(k), on the other hand, has an additional profit-sharing allowance built in that allows you to contribute another $29,000 per year. And these numbers are per-person, so if you and your spouse own and work in a business together, you can contribute up to $98,000 *per year* to a Solo 401(k).

One caveat here: you do have to earn the money first! If you and your spouse own and operate an S Corporation, for example,

Michael started selling collectibles and used merchandise on eBay after he graduated from college and couldn't find a job. It paid the bills and kept him afloat through some lean times. Even after he found a job Michael kept his eBay business going. But now, instead of spending that extra income, he created a Solo 401(k) plan for his eBay business and began putting his profits in there instead. It was a simple and easy way for Michael to save money for his retirement while lowering his tax bill at the same time.

If you're interested in learning more about how easy it is to set up and run an eBay business from your home, read *Tax Loopholes for eBay Sellers*, by Diane Kennedy and Janelle Elms. Go to www.reirallc.com for a free excerpt from this book.

you must each take a salary out of that S Corporation which is equal to your yearly contribution. You can't have a salary of $10,000 on the books and yet claim a $15,000 contribution.

You can't count profit distributions as salary, either—they would be allocated to the $29,000 profit sharing allowance you get each year. So if you're in the habit of taking a small salary and a large distribution from your S Corporation, you may need to change things a little before this plan can work to peak effectiveness.

A Solo 401(k) plan is a self-directed plan, meaning that you control where your money is invested. That opens up a *huge* array of possibilities—from buying real estate, to operating a restaurant, to investing in start-up ventures. You can even invest in some areas that have traditionally been forbidden to many traditional plans, such as life insurance and S corporations.

And here's something else—you can borrow from your Solo 401(k). The limits are $50,000 or up to 50 percent of the balance of your plan (as long as that 50 percent is under $50,000). Not only that, if your plan needs to borrow money (for instance, if it wants to purchase some real estate and doesn't have enough for an all-cash purchase), you can do so, without triggering something called "Unrelated Business Income Tax," or UBIT (more on UBIT in Chapter 14).

Setting up a Solo 401(k) plan is fairly straightforward. You need to first find an outside plan administrator or custodian (we have some resources for you at our web site, www.reirallc.com), and discuss your needs with them. You'll also need to decide whether you want to go it entirely alone, and be in charge of your investment decisions, or whether you want your custodian to manage that aspect as well. If you decide to self-manage your plan, you'll need to set up a business structure to operate within, because you can't play with your pension funds directly. Then you'll need to fund your plan, and off you go!

What we really like about this plan (besides the increased contribution amount) is the aspect of control. You aren't being given a list of approved mutual funds or stocks to buy into, nor are you being coerced to investing only in your employer's stock because they won't match funds otherwise. If you need help with investment decisions, you can get it—you're not left on your own to muddle through.

If that sounds good, then the next new plan—the Solo Roth 401(k)—is even better.

SOLO ROTH 401(K)

The Solo Roth 401(k) was also created a few years back, but it only came into force on January 3, 2006. It's actually a Solo 401(k) plan with a Roth component. In other words, all of the same Solo 401(k) requirements apply: You must be self-employed, receive 1099 income, or run a small business with only yourself and your spouse as full-time employees. You must set it up through an outside administrator who will act as the custodian, and choose to either self-direct the plan through a separate business structure or to have the plan managed by the administrator.

That's because what you're really doing is setting up a Solo 401(k) plan and then adding a Roth component to it. You can make contributions to one side or the other throughout the year—but you do need to specify that all contributions to your Solo Roth 401(k) plan are being made irrevocably—in other words you can't change your mind in a few months and swap them over to your Solo 401(k) instead. It is the administrator's job to make sure the amounts being paid into each side are recorded properly and kept separately, and to prepare the required reports for the IRS.

Another thing to bear in mind is that the Solo Roth 401(k) portion can only be funded with your salary income, and not your profit sharing. So although you can sock away up to $44,000 per year into your plan, only $15,000 of that $44,000 can go into the Roth 401(k) side—the $29,000 in profit sharing has to go into your Solo 401(k) side as deferred tax contributions. Of course, there's nothing that says it *has* to go there—you can always fund a Roth IRA first and then dump what's left into your Solo 401(k).

Hey Late Starters! Once you turn 50 you have a catch-up contribution allowance of an additional $5,000 per person, per year. That means you can make salary contributions of $20,000 each year, plus the $29,000 profit-sharing component, for a total of $49,000— or $98,000 if your spouse can contribute the maximum as well!

Once you've funded your Solo Roth 401(k), make sure you keep your funds in place for five years. This way, all of the money that comes out of the Solo Roth 401(k) plan comes out tax-free.

WHY THE SOLO 401(K) AND SOLO ROTH 401(K) BEAT THE REST

These two plans are so loaded with benefits it's hard to see why you'd choose to put your money anywhere else. Let's do a quick recap.

- There are no income limitations! You can make a ton of money and finally be able to use the fantastic tax opportunities a Roth fund provides. The Solo Roth 401(k) has no income limitation.
- You can finally put away a significant amount into a Roth fund, where it can grow tax-free. Instead of a $4,000 limit ($5,000 if you're over 50) in 2006 you now have $15,000 per year ($20,000 if you're over 50) to work with in 2006.
- You can use your tax-free Roth funds to invest in things that were previously prohibited, such as S Corporation stock and life insurance policies.
- You can borrow up to $50,000 or 50 percent of your plan's value (up to $50,000).
- While a mandatory distribution requirement kicks in with all of the traditional plans, including a Roth IRA, and even your Solo 401(k), there is no mandatory distribution requirement for your Solo Roth 401(k). What a great way to leave tax-free money to your kids!

Here's one more benefit: if you are using your pension funds to invest in real estate or small businesses, you can invest your Roth IRA, your Solo 401(k), Solo Roth 401(k), and all of your traditional IRAs (including SEP IRAs) into the same or multiple properties. If you've collected a bunch of small plans from previous jobs, and don't feel like paying any penalties to roll them over or convert them into a Roth IRA, this is a great way to consolidate them.

So if you and your spouse are both high income earners and you've maxed out your other tax-deferred options, this is your chance to shelter up to $98,000 *per year*. This is an absolutely incredible deal and we both believe that the Solo Roth 401(k) plans will prove to be one of, if not *the* most popular pension tool ever.

Travis and Peggy had lived a good life with a few investments, but not many. They both had good jobs until they left to start their own business when they were in their fifties. It's hard to say what exactly woke them up to their financial situation. But suddenly both of them realized that there was a major problem looming on their frontier. They didn't have enough of a retirement fund built up to support them in the lifestyle in which they wanted to become accustomed.

Travis had an interest in real estate and had actually done a couple of small fix and flips in the recent past. He'd made about $20,000 on each of the last two. They were interested in exploring how to do those now in their pension plan. The problem was they simply didn't have enough in their pension plan to start the plan.

Travis and Peggy thought that their only solution was to do the fix and flip properties in their own name and pay the tax.

That's when they discovered that they could start putting more away in their pension plan under the catch up provisions. In fact, they could put up to $98,000 per year away and it would allow them to have tax-deferred and tax-free income from their current wealth-building real estate strategies. Then later, they could take distributions from the fund after they'd sold or closed down their business. That meant there would be a lower tax rate for the retirement fund distributions.

SECTION THREE

Putting Your Money to Work

Chapter 7

MORE SECRETS YOUR FINANCIAL PLANNER NEVER TOLD YOU

So far we've been discussing creating a retirement fund. But once you've done that, and you have some pension funds under your belt, then what?

There are two parts to building your retirement fund. The first secret is getting some money into your fund. If you're a big spender, that might take some discipline, and possibly some spending cutbacks. If you're a lower to moderate income earner, it might mean starting a side business to help create income you can invest in your pension. In either case, the critical point is getting money into your pension. Fail to do that, and there won't be anything to build an investment strategy on.

The second step is just as important. It's not enough to just put money away for your retirement and hope that somehow magically it will grow into a nice nest egg so you can someday tell your boss, "Good Bye!" and spend your retirement living your dream life. You've got to invest that money so it can grow. We mentioned earlier that you'll need a nest egg of around $1.3 million to retire on a pension of $60,000 per year. As you aren't realistically going to save that much, the shortfall between what you do save and what you wind up with *has* to come from somewhere. But where?

There are a lot of financial planners and stockbrokers who can provide advice on how to invest your hard-saved money into traditional investments such as stocks and bonds. Some of these investment advisors can help you make some money, as long as you closely follow their plan and either start very early in saving money or are prepared to dramatically reduce your ideal retirement dream. But what they may not tell you about are secrets that can turn an ordinary retirement fund into a brand new lifestyle. In this chapter, we're going to explore five of our favorite investment strategies to help you grow your pension dramatically.

SECRET 1: USE A REAL SELF-DIRECTED PLAN

We've already talked about Secret 1. Self-directing your retirement fund is absolutely fundamental to taking control of its growth. The secret is to use a truly self-directed plan.

A self-directed IRA is legally no different from any other IRA. The term "self-directed" means simply that you choose your IRA's investments. But not all self-directed plans are created equal. Most brokerage houses and banks offer a "self-directed" plan. However, investments for these bank and brokerage sponsored plans are often limited to what the bank or brokerage house offers. In other words, they're self-directed—as long as you don't mind choosing from a preselected list of investments.

But nowadays Americans are demanding better solutions than the same old retirement investment options. Recent economic downturns like the dot.com (or dot.bomb, if you prefer) bust, business scandals, mutual fund scandals and so on have created huge losses in retirement accounts. Retirement accounts lost a total of $1.7 trillion from 2000 to 2004, and that has been the end of a retirement dream for many Americans. So now American investors are looking for other options, and not accepting the status quo of investment answers any longer.

At the same time that investors are demanding more control and better returns, their advisors, such as CPAs and attorneys, are attempting to backpedal on nontraditional investments. This isn't really that surprising. America is a litigious country, and most professionals have seen their malpractice insurance skyrocket in recent years. One attorney friend of Diane's told her that his law firm's malpractice premium went from $5,000 to $25,000 in a single year, without one claim being filed—solely because one of the attorneys was practicing securities law in the post-corporate-scandal world. As a professional, it is oftentimes safer to go with the known than take the risk of being sued by an irate client who took your advice to try something outside the box and it didn't work out.

It's also quite possible that your trusted advisors have never heard that it's perfectly legal to buy real estate or invest in businesses with your IRA. The ability to self-direct and invest your IRAs has been around for a long time, but it's only recently that more people are becoming aware of the possibilities.*

---

*Over the years we've found some amazing financial planners who recommend real estate as part of an overall investment scheme. We've assembled our lists into a single Rolodex that you can find at our web site, www.reirallc.com.

Grady was in his mid-fifties when he did a calculation for planning his retirement. He had limited confidence in whether he'd ever collect much in the way of Social Security. At best, he'd get about $1,400 per month from Social Security. His current house payment was more than that. And that didn't provide for medical insurance, medical expenses, utilities, food and the other things that provide just a basic level of living. He had some money in an IRA that was earning less than 3 percent per year. At that rate, he'd never be able to quit working. That's when Grady learned about self-directed IRAs.

Grady could be an ideal candidate for self-directed IRAs provided he also built up the skills to make money through his own investing. Otherwise, he could be putting his meager retirement funds at even more risk through his own mismanagement.

The moral of this story is that using a self-directed IRA fund gives you the ability to manage your funds. It's simply a tool to get rich, and get rich faster as you get income in the best tax-advantaged way. If you don't have the skills necessary to create income from the funds, it really won't matter.*

---

*Do your investing skills need honing? There are a lot of people in the market today who would love to take your money and teach you how to invest. What works and what doesn't? We've reviewed some of the most popular real estate gurus. What did we find that works and doesn't work? Go to www.reirallc.com for some objective feedback.

Even the IRS Is Confused

You have been able to buy real estate and invest in businesses with IRAs since the day they were created. However, if you called the IRS today and asked them if you could invest in real estate, you might be told "no." That same confusion that exists among financial planners also includes IRS employees.

Yet, take a look at IRS Publication 590,* *Individual Retirement Arrangements (IRAs)*, a 100-page IRS booklet that discusses pensions. Turn to pages 40–41. You'll see a list of what you can't do with an IRA. Those are called "prohibited transactions," and we'll be covering them in more detail a little later. But real estate *isn't* on the list, nor is investing in a small, private business. However, there are steps you must follow to do it right.

SECRET 2: PROTECT YOUR HARD-WORKING FUNDS

You can control your investments by self-directing the funds, but there are a couple more steps involved when you go this route. First, you'll need to find a custodian to hold your pension assets and administer your pension funds so that you stay in compliance with the IRS rules regarding pension plans. However, not all custodians are created equal.

What follows is our checklist of the seven things you should look for when auditioning custodians for your self-directed pension plan.

Checklist Item 1: Will the custodian allow you to invest in real estate and business?

The answer should be "yes." In fact, if you get a "no," that's a sure sign this custodian will limit your ability to self-direct your pension and will probably insist that you invest only in those products the custodian will make money on.

Checklist Item 2: Is your proposed custodian government-regulated?

All pensions must be held by an entity that is a bank, credit union, trust company, savings and loan, or an entity that

---

*You can find a link to IRS Publication 590 on our web site, www.reirallc.com.

is licensed and regulated by the IRS as a nonbank custodian. Individuals and organizations that don't meet these criteria are not permitted by law to hold IRA assets. To verify that your proposed custodian is regulated, ask for evidence like a bank charter document or regulatory contact information. Some IRA administrators use other financial institutions as the custodian. Only the actual custodian is subject to regulatory oversight. This means the administrator has no one watching to make sure they comply with the IRS regulations.

Here's why having a government-regulated custodian is so important: if you transfer your pension fund to a custodian who is not qualified (and unfortunately, there are some of them out there), the IRS will rule that the amount has been distributed. If that happens, all money in your pension fund will become taxable, just as though you had liquidated your pension and withdrawn all of the money. If you're under age 59½ when this happens, you'll get to pay a penalty, too.

Checklist Item 3: How much malpractice insurance does your proposed custodian have?

You've got a lot riding on the knowledge and experience of your custodian. When it comes to pension plans, the IRS is *very* unforgiving if you don't follow the rules. If something goes wrong—if your custodian steers you into trouble instead of out of it—are you covered? Make sure you examine your proposed custodian's paperwork closely to ensure you have the right to hold them accountable if something goes wrong.

Checklist Item 4: Who are your proposed custodian's auditors? What does their last audited financial statement show?

Custodian companies are required to be audited each year. As a part of your review and selection process, ask for a copy of the most recent audited financial statements, and the auditor's report that should accompany those statements. Read it carefully, and make a note if the auditors have included any exceptions or concerns in their opinion.

Checklist Item 5: Does your proposed custodian offer ongoing client education?

The best custodians want educated customers. Any education that's offered shouldn't be just a sales pitch, but should instead provide real information. Pension investing isn't well known or understood; there's plenty that the general population doesn't know. One of our strongly held beliefs is that education leads to better decisions.

Checklist Item 6: Ask about standard operating procedures and time requirements for new account set-up, transfers, purchases, sales, funding, distributions, IRS reporting, statement productions, and phone contacts.

The reason you're setting up a self-directed plan is so that you can work your plan's assets. That means there will be a lot of paperwork, due to the IRS's requirements for pension investments. How timely is your proposed custodian's response? Will you be constantly waiting for your custodian to catch up to your investment directives? Do they get all IRS-required filings done on time? Is your custodian going to be a help or a hindrance with the paperwork?

Checklist Item 7: How much are your proposed custodian's fees?

There is definitely a cost associated with having a custodian for your self-directed pension. Some custodians charge a flat

Diane's Story

I learned the hard way how much the wrong custodian could cost me. My husband and I have self-directed our IRAs for years. The investments grow tax deferred or tax-free because we use our IRA or Roth IRA funds. And, because we self-direct, we're able to control the investments and make even more money.

One of our investments through my husband's Roth IRA (set up in a year where we purposely drove down our income so we could get Roths established) was an IPO. It went public, and the stock shot up in value. Our stock was not restricted, so we were able to immediately sell and get a return of tenfold over what we had invested. We thought our only problem was that we'd only invested $5,000 (to return $50,000) instead of thousands more! That is until we tried to get our custodian to return our calls so we could get the stock sold. It took weeks to get them to return our frantic phone calls. Now we had to try to motivate them to quickly get into action. We waded through the paperwork they sent, completed it, and mailed it back. They lost it. Luckily, we had kept a copy and so we faxed over another copy. They wouldn't work off of a fax, so we had to overnight papers again. They lost the second set. Finally, after three weeks, we received the authorization to sell our own stock from the funds that we were self-directing. Meanwhile the stock price had plummeted to just over $22,000. We lost over $28,000 due to the inefficient way the custodian worked.

We are now very careful in how we screen the custodians who handle our self-directed funds. We never want to repeat that mistake again!*

---

*For a peek inside Diane's private list of advisors who understand self-directed IRAs, please go to www.reirallc.com.

fee, while others charge a fee based on a percentage of plan assets. That's because a custodian that lets you truly self-direct your funds doesn't usually make any commissions off of your investments. A bank or stock brokerage house, on the other hand, does make fees from investments you make off their list of approved investments. These custodians don't need to charge you an annual fee because they're making their profit off you in other ways. So when you're comparing custodians make sure to ask about and compare all hidden costs as well.

Custodian Checklist

Checklist Item 1: Will the custodian allow you to invest in real estate and business?

Checklist Item 2: Is your proposed custodian government-regulated?

Checklist Item 3: How much malpractice insurance does your proposed custodian have?

Checklist Item 4: Who are your proposed custodian's auditors? What does their last audited financial statement show?

Checklist Item 5: Does your proposed custodian offer ongoing client education?

Checklist Item 6: Ask about standard operating procedures and time requirements for new account set-up, transfers, purchases, sales, funding, distributions, IRS reporting, statement productions, and phone contacts.

Checklist Item 7: How much are your proposed custodian's fees?

SECRET 3: ROLL YOUR EXISTING PENSION FUNDS THE RIGHT WAY

There are plenty of rules about how you can roll over your existing pension funds into self-directed funds. If you've made the decision to roll over your existing pension funds into a self-directed plan, make sure you know what you need to know to keep you safe.

Rolling Funds Over from a Non-IRA Plan

The most common source of IRA funds are the orphan 401 (k) and 403 (b) plans that accumulate when we leave a job. Most fund administrators give you a choice of rolling the funds over or keeping them invested. In fact, in the rush of leaving, we've found a significant number of clients who just went off and left the funds sitting there. Without any orders to the contrary, the administrator will just keep the funds. Take an inventory of past jobs that you've had. Did you leave any retirement funds behind? Examples of non-IRA plans include: 401(k), 403(b), qualified annuity, profit sharing, defined benefit, money purchase, government-eligible deferred compensation, and Keogh plans. To roll funds over from these types of plans you'll need to:

- Select your self-directed plan custodian.
- Contact the self-directed plan custodian and complete all necessary paperwork to set up an account.
- Contact your current plan administrator and begin the rolling-over process.
- Generally your current plan's administrator will have a form for you to complete.

Note: The administrator may also offer to give you a check directly from the non-IRA plan. If you accept the check, you'll need to deposit it into a self-directed plan within 60 days or pay a penalty.

Rolling Funds Over from an IRA

If your funds are currently in a traditional IRA, you have a few roll-over options.

Option 1: Cash rollover transfer.

This is a faster transfer but will require some diligence on your part. You will actually receive a cash distribution from your old IRA and then endorse the distribution check over to your new custodian for the self-directed fund. You must do this within 60 days, or you'll be subject to tax on the amount you're rolling over plus penalties. To do a cash rollover, you'll need to:

1. Select your new self-directed plan custodian and complete all necessary paperwork to set up an account.
2. Request a cash distribution check from your current IRA custodian.
3. Endorse the payout check over to your new custodian. Complete all necessary paperwork required by your new custodian to accept the rollover.

Option 2: Direct Rollover.

A direct rollover moves your funds from an existing IRA directly to the new self-directed IRA. To do a direct rollover you'll need to:

1. Select your new self-directed plan custodian and complete all necessary paperwork to set up an account.
2. Contact your current IRA custodian and request that it transfer your funds to your new self-directed account.

Option 3: Conversion to Roth IRA.

Regardless of whether you start from a self-directed IRA, a non-IRA pension or a traditional IRA, when you're converting from a tax-deferred plan to a tax-free plan you will have some similar requirements. To do a simultaneous rollover and conversion you'll need to:

1. Check with your tax advisor to make sure you are eligible to make this type of conversion.*
2. Select your new self-directed Roth plan custodian and complete all necessary paperwork to set up an account.
3. Contact your current IRA custodian and request that your pension funds be transferred.
4. Pay the tax on the funds transferred. Since the money in the tax-deferred plan was not taxed when you paid it in, you will now have to pay the tax upon conversion to a Roth IRA.

SECRET 4: STAY LEGAL—AVOID PROHIBITED TRANSACTIONS, DISQUALIFIED PERSONS, AND PROHIBITED INVESTMENTS

Prohibited transactions are types of investments that you can't do. Disqualified persons are people that you can't use your pension funds to invest for or with. Prohibited investments are things you can't invest in. In other words, these three categories—prohibited transactions, disqualified persons and prohibited investments—are all things you must avoid with your self-directed

---

*Tax law is constantly changing. Please visit www.reirallc.com to review the current IRS requirements for conversions from non-Roth to Roth plans. As of 2006, there are income limitations on conversions.

funds, or risk huge tax penalties. Let's take a look at all three of these in more detail.

Prohibited Transactions

Prohibited transactions include:

- The sale, exchange or lease of any property between a plan and a disqualified person.
- The furnishing of goods, services, or facilities between a plan and a disqualified person.
- Using any portion of your pension fund as security for a loan by a disqualified person.
- Use of income or assets of a plan by a disqualified person for her own benefit.

So far, everything we've discussed is straight out of IRC Section 408 and the Treasury Regulations related to that section. But while prohibited transactions are fairly straightforward, there is a little confusion when it comes to exactly defining who a disqualified person could be.

Disqualified Persons

The definition of a disqualified person includes the owner of the plan and any beneficiary of the plan. So, for example, Diane has a pension plan that lists her husband and her son as beneficiaries. That means that Diane, her husband Richard, and son David are all disqualified persons in relation to Diane's pension plan.

Depending on how you interpret IRC Section 4975, a disqualified person can also be a family member who isn't listed as a beneficiary. For example, this rather unclear Code Section seems to indicate that your children might be considered disqualified, even if you disinherited them from your pension.

The safest route is to say that any direct-line relative would be disqualified (parents, grandparents, or children), whereas a sibling is not, unless he or she is listed as a beneficiary. So, while you can't enter into a sale, exchange, or lease of a property between your plan and one of your parents or one of your children, you can do these transactions with your brothers and sisters, unless, of course, they are listed as beneficiaries.

Prohibited Investments

This is a very short list! Prohibited investments include:

- Collectibles such as art, rugs, antiques, metal, gems, stamp, coins, alcoholic beverages, or other tangible personal property
- Life Insurance

Things You Can't Do with A Real Estate Transaction

Now that you have an idea of what general prohibited transactions for pension investments look like, let's take a look at some specific issues you may run into with your real estate pension investments.

Your pension cannot directly or indirectly buy real estate from a disqualified person. In this case, disqualified persons include:

- You, as the pension's owner.
- Your children or your parents.
- Your sons- or daughters-in-law.
- Your pension fund's custodian, trustee, anyone providing services to your pension fund or otherwise considered a fiduciary.
- An entity that is owned at least 50 percent (directly or indirectly) by a combination of the disqualified persons set out

above (for instance, if you and your spouse own 50 percent of an LLC, that LLC becomes a disqualified person).

- Any officer, director, 10 percent (or more) shareholder, or any highly compensated employees of such an entity.

You can't have your pension fund enable an investment for you or another disqualified person. In other words, if the IRS views your pension fund's investment as essential to accomplishing a transaction in which both you and your IRA invest, then the transaction would be considered a prohibited transaction.

Diane's Story

One client I'll always remember was a doctor who really thought he knew more than his advisors and the custodian for his company's pension plan. Even though it wasn't supposed to be self-directed, he was somehow able to access the company's million-dollar pension plan. And, he self-directed it—right into huge penalties. He decided that diamonds would make a great investment. Even if he had been able to self-direct the fund, he still couldn't have invested in gems. There aren't a lot of prohibited investments, but the rules are very clear for the ones that are listed on the "don't do" list.

Suddenly the pension plan was faced with a huge 50 percent excise tax penalty (that meant a penalty of $500,000 for the $1,000,000 fund). Even worse, the doctor could easily have faced criminal penalties because it wasn't his money to invest in the first place.

Pension plans have a lot of rules. If you play by the rules, your wealth will grow even faster than if you invested with regular after tax money. But you have to play by the rules. There are huge penalties if you do not.

Your pension fund can't purchase a piece of real estate and then have a disqualified person use it while it is owned by your pension. For example, you can't buy a vacation home and use it partly for personal use, even though you might rent it to unrelated persons the rest of the year.

Things You Can't Do with Business Investing

When your pension fund invests in an enterprise with which you currently have or in the future will have some other relationship—such as being a current owner, co-investor, employee, creditor, director or officer—there is often a question of whether that investment is prohibited.

If a prohibited transaction between you and your pension happens, your pension will become subject to an immediate tax. That tax will be based on the entire value of your pension! So in other words, one wrong move and you'll have to pay tax on your entire pension fund.

Prohibited transaction issues can also arise after you've made an investment. This usually happens in connection with a transaction or service that happens between your pension and a disqualified company, a disqualified person, or you.

Unfortunately, there aren't any clear-cut rules from the government or the courts on rules regarding an IRA investment in a closely held enterprise. Because the rules are still being developed, we don't know what specifically can be called a prohibited transaction. However, our research has left us with some general observations.

- In an advisory opinion, the Department of Labor (the government agency that interprets prohibited transaction rules) decided that where an IRA and the IRA's owner both invested in a partnership, it would not be considered prohibited if the IRA's owner and his family together held less than 50 percent of the partnership, and the IRA's owner didn't receive any direct or indirect benefit (such as a job with the partnership). In this instance "family" did not include brothers or sisters of the IRA's owner. This appears to say that you can co-invest with your IRA in certain circumstances, as long as you follow the Department of Labor's requirements to the letter.

- We know that when a pension invests in a business in which the pension fund's owner and his or her direct relatives already own 50 percent or more, the transaction will be considered prohibited. However, many financial advisors believe that if you, your direct relatives, *and* your pension fund all invest in the business simultaneously at the very beginning of the business's existence (in other words, as soon as it is incorporated), that transaction won't be considered prohibited. You're going to want legal advice on this one, though, and it would also be a good idea to make sure that your attorney or formation service understands *exactly* what you are trying to do so that all shareholdings are issued simultaneously, and at the right time.

- Your pension can't invest in a business where part of the deal involves the business giving you a personal benefit. For example, your pension can't invest in a business on the basis that you get a job with that business, nor can your pension fund threaten to withdraw its investment if you aren't given a job or allowed to keep a job.

Prohibited Transaction Examples

Here are some real-life examples we got from IRC 4975.

Prohibited Transaction Example 1: An IRA owns at least 50 percent of a company. Can the IRA invest more money in the same company?

Prohibited Transaction Answer 1: No; no further investments, capital contributions, loans, stock purchases can be done with IRA funds.

Prohibited Transaction Solution 1: If the pension (alone or together with certain related persons) owned less than 50 percent of the company, it would be allowed to make further sales or exchanges at arms-length.

Prohibited Transaction Example 2: An IRA owns 70 percent of a corporation or an LLC. Can that IRA's owner add more money personally if the company needed additional capital?

Prohibited Transaction Answer 2: Probably, if an independent person approved the additional contribution.

Prohibited Transaction Solution 2: To be more certain that this transaction would be permitted, use a loan from an outside source. This way, your pension's ownership percentage will remain the same and the business can get the working capital it needs to survive.

SECRET 5: MAKE SMART USE OF THE AVAILABLE OPTIONS

For our last secret, let's take a look at all of the things that you *can* do with your pension fund. And, boy, are there a lot of opportunities here! The IRS tells us what we can't do, not what we can do, when it comes to pension investing. The law that pertains to pension investments is an exclusive list, not an inclusive one. In other words, if the law doesn't say "don't do it," then you can safely assume that you can. That means permitted investments could include:

- Mutual Funds.
- Stocks.

- Bonds.
- Certificates of Deposit.
- Private Placements in unregistered companies.
- Limited Liability Company membership interests.
- Limited Partnership Interests.
- C Corporation Stock.
- Promissory Notes.
- Trust Deeds (or Mortgages).
- Real Property.
- Much More!

Jason bought a single-family home at the market price of $250,000 through his self-directed IRA. He had enough cash to purchase the property outright, so he didn't bother with a mortgage.

Jason bought the property with the intention of selling it to his brother, Neal. He would accomplish this by having Neal buy the house from his pension fund at the fair market value of $250,000. Neal would make a small down payment to Jason's pension fund and would receive a mortgage from Jason's pension fund over the rest of the property that he would pay back over time.

This is an example of a permitted transaction that created a win-win solution for everyone! Jason was able to help his brother buy a home, when Neal might not otherwise have qualified for a mortgage. Plus, Jason now has a guaranteed rate of return for his IRA.

Chapter 8

DISTRIBUTIONS FROM YOUR PENSION FUND

I f all goes well, you're going to have made a lot of money with your pension fund. You'll bypass Granny-on-the-Porch money and go straight to Bronzed Jet-Setter. And that's great! But you need to also plan for how you get that money back out of your pension, too. Remember, if you're working with tax-deferred money, the IRS will come looking for their share.

Sometimes you'll need to get at your money before you retire. Maybe you want to roll from a tax-deferred fund to a tax-free fund like a Roth IRA or a Solo Roth 401(k). Or maybe you have some unexpected expenses, some medical issues arise, and so forth. With most tax-deferred pensions, you will pay taxes as well as an early-distribution penalty to get that money back out. What you need here are some creative strategies to get your money out while avoiding penalties and taxes as much as possible.

TAX DEFERRED IRAS

A tax-deferred IRA is any form of the more traditional IRA. You received a tax deduction when you put money in the account, and it builds, tax deferred. Tax-deferred means tax later, and that day of reckoning happens when you take money out of the account.

TAXES DUE UPON DISTRIBUTION

Distributions from your tax-deferred IRA are taxed at your ordinary tax rate. That's the tax rate you pay on your earned income—the income from your job, interest you earn, or income from your business if you're self-employed. And, as you know, that income is taxed at a higher tax rate than the rate for long-term capital gains and for dividends. You can also find yourself subject to a 10 percent early distribution penalty when you take money out of your plan.

Now there's no way out of paying income tax on your distributions. That's just part of the deal you get when you do a tax-deferred plan. But there *are* ways to avoid that 10 percent early distribution penalty.

CONTRIBUTIONS RETURNED EARLY

If you make IRA contributions and then withdraw those contributions during the same year they were made, you can get your money out without paying tax on it if you make the withdrawal before filing your tax return. If you get an extension of time to file your tax return, you can withdraw your IRA contributions for that year tax-free by the extended due date. All you're really doing here is returning the contributions you made. Remember, as you haven't yet filed your tax return, you haven't yet received a tax-deferred benefit. So it's really just a wash in this case.

WHEN YOU MUST TAKE CONTRIBUTIONS

Sometimes you have to take money out of your tax-deferred plan, or risk paying extra taxes and penalties. This happens when (1) you've contributed too much money to your plan during the year, and (2) you've reached the age where you must start receiving minimum distributions.

EXCESS CONTRIBUTIONS

In some cases, you have to take back your contributions. That's true if you have put too much money into your plan (for example, you changed jobs during the year and your new salary didn't match the contribution amounts from your old job). If you don't take that extra money back out again you'll get stuck with having to pay a 6 percent excise tax. Remember as your income grows, some pension contribution amounts are reduced.

If you find yourself in the position of having to withdraw excess contributions, make sure you do this before your tax return is due. If you file an extension for your tax return's due date, then you have until the end of that extension to withdraw the extra money.

MINIMUM DISTRIBUTIONS

You cannot keep funds in an IRA forever. Eventually, they must be distributed. If the IRA fails to make the minimum distributions, it may be subject to a 50 percent excise tax. Yes, that's right—you could get hit with a tax equivalent to 50 percent of your IRA's value!

We're going to go through some of the rather convoluted rules for calculating the minimum distribution requirements. This is one case where you will want an expert's help, though. Your custodian or CPA should be able to help you calculate the minimum distributions required.

Your IRA must begin distributing by April 1 of the year following the year in which you reach age 70½. April 1 is referred to as the required beginning date.

You must receive at least a minimum amount for each year starting with the year in which you reach 70½ years old. If you do not receive that minimum in your 70½ year, then you must receive distributions for your 70½ year by April 1 of the next year. On the other hand, if you receive more than the required minimum distribution in one year, you don't get credit for the additional amount in future years.

FIGURING THE REQUIRED MINIMUM DISTRIBUTION

The IRS provides tables to determine the required minimum distribution in Publication 590.* There are some terms that are used in those tables that would be good to review.

IRA Account Balance: The IRA account balance is the amount in your IRA at the beginning of the year.

Contributions: For purposes of the minimum distribution calculation, disregard contributions made after the end of the previous year.

---

*You'll find a link to IRS Publication 590 on our web site, www.reirallc.com.

Distributions: Distributions reduce your IRA's account balance in the year they are made.

Distribution period: This is the maximum number of years over which the table shows you will take distributions from your IRA. The period to use is listed in Appendix C of Publication 590.

Life expectancy: The IRS provides actuarially determined life expectancy for your age. This is also provided in Appendix C. If you have a spouse, you will also have to calculate your spouse's life expectancy, using these tables.

Distributions during your life: After going through all the previous definitions and factors, your required minimum distributions during your lifetime are then calculated using the table for singles, table for joint or table for joint where your spouse is more than 10 years younger.

It's confusing enough to read, let alone apply. That's why we don't recommend you try to go through this formula by yourself. If you make a mistake and don't take enough out, remember the penalty is a 50 percent excise tax. However, it is good to mark your calendar for the date when you need to start making the calculation and taking distributions.

BENEFICIARY OF AN IRA

If you are a surviving spouse who is the sole beneficiary of your spouse's IRA, you may choose to be considered the owner, not the beneficiary. That means the calculations for the minimum distributions will be based on your information. Additionally, if you elect to be treated as a beneficiary, or if you actually are a beneficiary and not a surviving spouse, you may be required to take out the entire balance of the IRA by the fifth year following the year of the original IRA owner's death.

TAXABLE DISTRIBUTIONS

Generally, distributions from a traditional IRA are taxable and subject to early withdrawal penalties in the year you receive them. This is true even if you receive a distribution you didn't request or want, such as from a failed financial institution.

There are some exceptions. The following distributions are not subject to early withdrawal penalties:

- Distributions on or after the date in which the taxpayer is $59\frac{1}{2}$.
- Distributions after the taxpayer's death.
- Distributions on account of the taxpayer's disability.
- Distribution in the form of substantially equal periodic payments for the life or life expectancy of the owner.
- Distributions due to hurricane damage.
- Distribution due to medical expenses that are in excess of 7.5 percent of adjusted gross income.
- Distribution due to unemployment for over 12 weeks.
- Distributions to pay for qualified higher education expenses for taxpayer, taxpayer's spouse, child, or grandchild.
- Distributions for first-time home buyer ($10,000 limitation).

TAXABLE AND NONTAXABLE IRAS

You might have made contributions to your IRA that were nondeductible. Prior to Roth IRAs, it was possible, and in fact, sometimes even a good idea, to make nondeductible IRA contributions. In some cases, these nondeductible IRAs were commingled with deductible IRAs in the same fund. Now, it's time to distribute. That means you'll need to make a separate calculation if part of your IRA was nondeductible. Some of the IRA funds will be taxable (the part that was deductible) and some will be nontaxable (the part that was nondeductible).

Remember if all of your IRA was deductible, then the entire

amount is tax-deferred, and that means you'll pay tax on all of it. A calculation only needs to be made if you have mixed deductible and nondeductible contributions in the same account.

The part of the distribution that represents nondeductible contributions is tax-free. Distributions of the income and the deductible contributions will be taxable. Now here is where it gets even more complicated. You can't select whether your distribution is taxable or nontaxable. You have to make a calculation of how much will be taxable on each contribution you receive.

LOSS ON TRADITIONAL IRA

What if your IRA has lost money? Well, there is some relief available to you, but not a lot. If you have a loss within your traditional

Awbry made a $2,000 nondeductible contribution to her IRA. So, her basis is, thus, $2,000. During the year, Awbry's IRA earned $400, and she took out a distribution of $600.

Awbry would pay tax on only one-sixth of her $600 distribution. This would be calculated as the taxable amount, divided by the total amount. In Awbry's case that means ($400/($2000 + $400)). The rest of her distribution is nontaxable. So, Awbry would pay tax on $100 and would receive $500 as a return of capital.

The next year Awbry's IRA loses $500. At the end of the year, her IRA's balance is $1,300. That was calculated as her original $2,000 plus the interest of $400 she made last year, less the distribution of $600 she took out last year and less the loss of $500 her IRA had this year. Awbry's basis is $1,500. This is calculated as her nondeductible contribution of $2,000 less the return-of-capital portion of $500 that she received in the previous year. So when tax time comes this year, Awbry will have a deductible loss of $200, which is the difference between the IRA balance of $1,300 and Awbry's basis of $1,500. (Does anyone still dispute the need for accountants?)

IRA, you can recognize that loss (take a deduction) on your tax return, but only after all the amounts in *all* of your traditional IRA accounts have been distributed to you. Plus, the total distributions need to be less than your unrecovered basis (your basis is the total amount of the nondeductible contributions in your traditional IRAs). In a second, we'll go through an example that will help to show how this might work. That loss will be shown as a miscellaneous itemized deduction on Schedule A, subject to 2 percent of adjusted gross income.

If you have a deductible IRA, however, you can't recognize a loss. You took a deduction when you originally contributed money to that IRA and, although it has lost money, it's money you would have paid tax on when you received it anyway.

SO, WHEN CAN YOU TAKE A DISTRIBUTION?

Finally, after we've worked through some of the other details, we get to the question that started this whole chapter. When can you take a distribution? Or maybe a better question is "When can you take a distribution and not have to pay the 10 percent penalty?"

AFTER AGE 59½ AND BEFORE AGE 70½

After you reach age 59½, you can receive distributions without having to pay the 10 percent additional tax. You're not required to take distributions until you reach age 70½, however.

But sometimes that's not true. Remember the Solo Roth 401(k) plan doesn't require you to take distributions at all, no matter how old you are.

DISTRIBUTIONS BEFORE AGE 59½

Generally, if you're less than age 59½ when you take your distribution, you'll pay a 10 percent additional tax as an early withdrawal penalty. Remember that you'll pay tax on the distributions (except as noted above) at any rate. This is an additional penalty. There are some exceptions, though. You may not have to pay the penalty if:

- You have unreimbursed medical expenses that are more than 7.5 percent of your adjusted gross income.
- The distributions are not more than the cost of your medical insurance.
- You are disabled.
- You are the beneficiary of a deceased IRA owner.
- You are receiving distributions in the form of an annuity.
- The distributions are not more than your qualified higher education expense.
- You use the distributions to buy, build, or rebuild a first home.

ROTH IRA DISTRIBUTIONS

There is no tax due on the contributions or earnings from the Roth account when you distribute the proceeds. The IRA is a tax-deferred investment vehicle. You do pay tax on everything, eventually. The contributions that go into a Roth are after tax, so you've paid the tax. But you never pay tax on the earnings within a Roth. That subtle difference can make all the difference in supercharging your investment.

You will, however, pay an early distribution tax penalty of 10 percent if you take distributions prior to age 59½ without meeting one of the exceptions above. You also cannot take a distribution during the first five years of your contributions. The exceptions stated for the IRAs above are the same exceptions to the penalty for Roth IRAs.

SUMMARY

Calculating the tax and penalty due on distributions can be complicated, especially if you have deductible and nondeductible commingled in the same account. That's why you need to have a qualified advisor helping you with this. Here are some numbers to review:

- Age 59½—distributions can be taken without penalty.
- Age 70½—minimum distributions required (unless you're using a Solo Roth 401(k).
- 5 years—length of time contributions must stay in a Roth prior to removal.

Strategies to Make Your Money Work Even Harder with Less Effort

Chapter 9

THE IRA OR TAX-FREE LLC: CONTROL FROM A DISTANCE

I n the last few chapters we talked about how you could use your pension money to invest in real estate or business ventures, and how investing "outside the box" of traditional stocks and mutual funds could make your pension grow higher and faster than you'd ever thought possible. One common element throughout the information you've been given so far is that whatever your pension plan, it needs to be self-directed to work most effectively.

But just because your pension plan is self-directed doesn't always mean you have full control. That's because most types of self-directed pension plans require you to have someone (or something) to act as a plan administrator (sometimes called a custodian or trustee). This person or company manages the back-end administration and the paperwork—making sure that things get filed with the IRS, that taxes get paid, and holds title to your assets. A good administrator can also help you make investment choices, and warn you when you're about to make a misstep into the murky depths of prohibited transactions.

Being self-directed can also slow things down. Remember back to one of Diane's earlier stories in Chapter 7, where she and her husband, Richard, had invested $5,000 in one company's stock that subsequently went public and shot up to $50,000—10 times its initial value. Diane and Richard wanted to sell before the price dropped back down, but problems at their administrator's end left them unable to communicate their instructions to their custodian until the stock value had dropped to about $22,000.

If you're planning on using your pension funds to invest in real estate, time can be, as they say, "of the essence." Even though many feel the housing market is cooling (that's good—it means better investment opportunities for the knowledgeable and serious real estate investor), there are still great deals out there—but oftentimes when you find that awesome deal you need to put money down right away to lock it up or lose the deal to another savvy real estate investor who's on the way over with a checkbook. If you have to call your plan administrator and arrange for a check to be written and delivered to you made out to the seller, you can pretty much guarantee a wait time of between 24–36 hours before you can lock up the property—in other words, plenty of time for someone else to come along and snare the deal out from under you.

Remember when we discussed prohibited transactions, disqualified persons, and prohibited investments? One of the problems occurred when your pension plan invested in something that would benefit you. That type of transaction is called "self-dealing." In other words, you and your pension plan are dealing with each other, both for the benefit of you personally. You can innocently fall into the trap of self-dealing by first being personally involved in a real estate deal.

For example, let's say you find a great deal on real estate and want to tie it up with a contract. You'll need to write and sign an offer, and write an earnest money check. So what do you do? You can't write a check from your personal funds and have your plan pay you back later. That'll drop you squarely into the self-dealing trap, and now you're prohibited from using pension funds to complete the purchase. Even if that first check is never cashed, simply by writing it, you've completely barred your pension plan from participating in the deal. You know that you can't contact your pension custodian, no matter how responsive they are, and have them instantaneously hand a check to you while you're sitting in the real estate agent's office.

But if you're a knowledgeable investor who has taken advantage of a brilliant new(ish) strategy that allows you to administer and self-direct your investments, all the while maintaining the safe distance that the IRS Code and Treasury Regulations require, you can still make the deal happen—today. That strategy is to use a limited liability company (LLC) in conjunction with your pension plan. We call this an IRA LLC, if you're using it with a deferred-tax pension plan or a Tax-Free LLC, if you're using the LLC together with a tax-free pension plan like a Roth IRA or a Solo Roth 401(k). How the LLC actually functions is the same for both types.

First let's take a quick look at what an LLC is, before taking a look at how it works, and why this strategy makes so much sense.

The real estate market was slowing in Yvette's home town of San Diego. The prices for perfect houses hadn't dropped much at all, but there were now deals that could be made with distressed sellers, especially if there was some deferred maintenance on the property.

Yvette had done her research on her pension plan. It was the main source of available funds to invest. She had rolled over a 401(k) from a previous employer and so had just a little over $100,000 she could use to invest with. She knew that if she got a loan with her pension that the best she could hope for was 70 percent LTV (loan to value). That meant that she needed to find a house in the $250,000 range. In many parts of San Diego, that would be pretty tough to find. After a lot of looking and some cold calling, she found a distressed seller with a condo in a great building. There was some updating needed, and, worst of all, there was a strong smell of animals in the place. Yvette knew how to update and clean the place up, and she knew she'd also make some good money on a flip.

But there were other interested buyers, and she needed to act quickly. The only money Yvette had was in her pension fund. Without that money, she couldn't afford the down payment, closing costs, and remodeling costs.

What are Yvette's options? If the pension is held directly with a qualified custodian, she'll need to request that the custodian write a check for the earnest money deposit. The property will be long gone by the time all that happens. If she writes the check for the earnest money deposit directly from her personal funds, she won't be able to access the pension funds for the property. Luckily, Yvette had thought ahead and formed an IRA LLC for her pension plan. She knew that there was specialized language required in the documents, and so she'd hired an expert to form the specialized IRA

LLC. She was the administrator for the LLC, so she could write the earnest money check directly from the LLC checking account. All was well and she could proceed with closing the property using the available funds in her pension plan. The LLC made it much easier to proceed with buying the property and moving quickly on the best deals.

LLCs IN A NUTSHELL

An LLC is a stand-alone legal entity that is a cross between a regular business corporation and a limited partnership. It is a full and separate legal entity in the eyes of the law. Invented in Germany, LLCs came into existence in the United States in the 1970s, as a way to combine all of the best features of a business corporation (e.g., tax deductions and legal status as a separate and distinct entity) and limited partnerships (e.g., asset protection and method of taxation).

In Germany, LLC's go by the tongue-twisting name of *Gesellschaft mit beschränkter Haftung* (limited liability company), or "GmbH."

Ownership in an LLC is held through membership interests, rather than the shares you'd receive in a corporation, and the owners of an LLC are called members instead of shareholders.

The management structure of an LLC is quite different from that of a corporation. Instead of being divided up into officers and directors (the way a corporation's management is set up) management in an LLC is handled in one of three ways:

1. By all of the members together.
2. By a select portion of the members.
3. By a third group, called managers.

The first two options are called member-managed LLCs, while the third option is called a manager-managed LLC.

An LLC's members are protected from liability, just as shareholders are. If an LLC goes bankrupt, its creditors cannot ask the members to make good on the LLC's debts. That same protection is extended to the management of an LLC. As long as the LLC's management has been acting honestly and in the best interests of the LLC, whether member-managed or manager-managed, the courts have consistently held that these individuals cannot be made personally liable for an LLC's debts.

One very important difference between LLCs and corporations is how members may legally protect their ownership interests from creditors. If you own shares in a corporation and go bankrupt or are sued and have a judgment made against you, your shares are at risk. A creditor or bankruptcy trustee can take those shares away from you and sell them. If you are the only owner of that corporation, or the majority shareholder of a corporation, a creditor or bankruptcy trustee can also vote to liquidate the assets of the corporation to satisfy their claim. But it's very different for LLC ownership interests. These cannot be seized by creditors or bankruptcy trustees without a special court order (in some states those interests may not be seized at all), which means the assets in the LLC remain safe as well. And favorable taxation rules mean that LLCs are one of, if not *the* best business structure to hold any form of appreciating assets in—from mutual funds and stock portfolios to real estate investments.

The combination of tax deductions and taxation treatment makes LLCs attractive from a business perspective, while the asset and liability protection LLCs receive makes them very attractive from a legal standpoint. Since their introduction, LLCs have quickly evolved into one of the premier business structures to hold assets and to operate passive business activities, such as collecting royalties from product licensing. LLCs are also *the* vehicle of choice in most states to hold real estate investments (limited partnerships may work better in some states where LLCs are subject to additional taxes). All of these advantages make them extremely attractive from a pension standpoint, particularly because your pension is growing and may contain several very valuable assets.

HOW AN IRA LLC WORKS

By creating an IRA LLC or a Tax-Free LLC to work with your pension plan, you create the ability to truly self-direct your plan. That's because your plan doesn't need to function exclusively through its administrator. It can now use the LLC to buy, sell, and manage your plan's assets.

The secret is to create a manager-managed LLC—anything else will run afoul of pension rules and will create problems. The LLC will have one member and one manager. Your pension plan will be the member, while you personally will be the manager.

Once you have set up your LLC, it can be funded by your pension plan. Your pension plan can choose how much it is going to invest in the LLC, and transfers that money into the LLC's operating account.

Now the LLC is free to go out and search for good investments. And because you are the manager of the LLC, you can control where it spends money and when. This time, when you find that incredible real estate deal that won't last, you can write a check from the LLC's bank account—because as the manager, you have signing authority on the bank account, as well as the authority to make business decisions on behalf of the LLC. In other words, you've got the same type of control that the president of a corporation has. This is often referred to as "checkbook control." Later, after you perform due diligence, if you still want to purchase the property, the LLC pays the down payment and closing costs. The LLC will be on title as the owner of the property, but the deed will be held by the plan administrator.

Do you see how this can work to your benefit? By using an LLC together with your pension plan, you've taken away that 24–36-hour wait period between asking your plan administrator to write a check for an asset and receiving that check.

So does all of this mean you can boldly strike out and do whatever you please with the LLC's money? No! Your pension plan's administrator still needs to know what you're doing—in fact, it's

Tabitha's Restaurant

Tabitha found a great deal on a restaurant that she wanted to buy with her brother and fund with her pension. Her brother would run the restaurant—Tabitha wanted to stay in the background. While she could have created a single LLC to operate the restaurant, owned partially by her IRA and partially by her brother, she decided to open two LLCs. Why? Because she wanted to do lots of things with her IRA LLC, and didn't want to take her brother along as a partial owner of everything. Her solution was to form an IRA LLC owned entirely by her pension, and a second LLC owned by her IRA LLC and her brother. Now the restaurant asset was protected, Tabitha's interests were protected, and her IRA LLC was free to invest in other business ventures as well.

more important than ever to involve your administrator. Because you are going entirely self-directed *and* self-controlled, your administrator will no longer be responsible for making sure all of your plan's transactions are done safely, within pension investing rules. That's the trade-off you make for complete control. However, a good plan administrator will be an excellent sounding board and, as long as you run the details by him ahead of time, will make sure to let you know if you're about to step over the line. Be careful here, though. If you don't discuss transactions ahead of time, or if you carry through on a transaction even after you've been told it could be considered prohibited, then your plan administrator won't be held responsible for the consequences—you will. And those consequences can be severe, and can include a significant fine as well as the dissolution of your pension plan.

SETTING UP YOUR IRA LLC

To summarize, if you want to set up an IRA LLC and use it to self-direct your investments you'll need to follow these steps:

1. Have a pension plan (consider rolling smaller plans into one big plan if you can do more by consolidating your funds).
2. Make sure your pension plan is administered by a custodian who understands both what you are trying to accomplish and who allows for truly self-directed investing.
3. Form a manager-managed LLC (we have some suggestions to get help with this on our web site, www.reirallc.com).
4. Locate a suitable asset (or assets) and review with your plan administrator to make sure the transaction is both worthwhile and permitted under your plan's rules.
5. Transfer funds from your pension fund to your IRA LLC so it can purchase the property.

6. Run the business or property through your IRA LLC, making sure that operating profit distributions flow back into your pension fund.
7. At some point in the future, sell the property and distribute the net gain back into your pension fund.

THE TAX-FREE LLC

Let's talk for a few minutes about the Tax-Free LLC, and the differences between it and the IRA LLC. In practical terms, a Tax-Free LLC is going to function almost exactly the same way that an IRA LLC works: manager-managed LLC, funded by your pension plan, with you calling the investing shots and your plan administrator making sure you don't break any rules by accident. But it does have some differences.

First of all, while an IRA LLC can be used with any type of tax-deferred pension plan, you can only use a Tax-Free LLC with a tax-free plan—in other words a Roth IRA or a Solo Roth 401(k).

There is one more tax that you're going to hear about in Chapter 14. That's called the UDFI or UBIT tax. For now, let's just say that once you hear about this tax, you'll really like the Solo Roth 401(k). That's because this tax, which only happens if you also borrow through your pension plan, does not apply to the Solo 401 (k) or Solo Roth 401 (k).

So if you also wanted to escape UDFI and UBIT, you would limit your pension plan choice even further, and use only a Tax-Free LLC combined with a Solo Roth 401(k). This special LLC takes advantage of the tax-free advantages of a Roth and combines it with the UDFI escape clause in a 401(k). We actually prefer this method rather than using a Roth IRA, because the Solo Roth 401(k) offers so many more benefits—you can fund it higher, grow it faster, and leave it to your kids without ever having to take a mandatory distribution. Add all that to the idea of not paying UDFI tax, and the result is a winning combination. This tax-free plan is also exempt from the dreaded AMT.

But to get started with a Tax-Free LLC, you're first going to need a tax-free plan. That means you either need to start a Solo Roth 401(k) plan or roll over existing Roth IRA funds into a Solo Roth 401(k) plan. You can also consider cross-funding and move tax-deferred pension funds, but there will be some tax consequences here, which we'll discuss in more detail in later chapters.

Here are the steps you'll need to take to set up and get rolling with a Tax-Free LLC:

1. The first step might be the toughest. That's because if you don't have a business, you're going to need to form one. For the Tax-Free LLC plan to truly work, and for you to still be able to leverage your money, you'll need a Solo Roth 401(k). And, as you'll recall, when we told you about the Solo Roth 401(k) plan back in Chapter 6 we said that it was still an employer-sponsored plan, meaning that you needed to be either self-employed, receive 1099 income, or operate your own full or part-time business with yourself and your spouse as the only full-time employees.

2. Set up your self-directed Solo Roth 401(k) plan. Use a recommended custodian who understands and supports what you're trying to do and offers both the Solo Roth 401(k) administration option and the self-directed LLC option.

3. Fund your new Solo Roth 401(k) plan. Roll other Roth plans into this fund, or consider whether taking a tax hit now to roll other, tax-deferred plans into this plan is worth the price in the long term.

4. Form a Tax-Free LLC to handle the administration. Again, make sure it is a manager-managed LLC with you named as manager and your Solo Roth 401(k) plan named as the member.

5. Locate a suitable asset (or assets) and review with your plan administrator to make sure the transaction is both worthwhile and permitted under your plan's rules.

6. Transfer funds from your Solo Roth 401(k) to your Tax-Free LLC so it can purchase the property.

7 Run the business or property through your Tax-Free LLC, making sure that operating profit distributions flow back into your Solo Roth 401(k).

8. Make sure you keep your Roth IRA or your Solo Roth 401(k) plan going for at least five years! Holding a Roth IRA or a Solo 401(k) plan for less than that can mean you lose the tax-free benefit and wind up paying tax on distributions down the road.

9. At some point in the future, sell the property and distribute the net gain back into your Solo Roth 401(k) where it will grow—tax-free.

CAUTIONS AND CAVEATS

While we really love both the IRA LLC and the Tax-Free LLC strategies, there are some things you need to be aware of before you put them into place.

Remember that the money you transfer from your pension plan to the LLC isn't a loan—it's an investment by your pension plan in a (hopefully) income-producing asset. It's really the same thing as taking money from your savings to buy a coffee shop. You have converted your liquid money into a hard asset. Now that you've converted your money, there are only two ways to get it back: first through the profits the coffee shop makes over time, and second, by selling the coffee shop at some point in the future for (hopefully) a profit.

Putting money into your LLC works the same way. You hope the LLC goes off and buys assets that will produce income, and flow that income back to your pension plan through profit distributions, and, maybe later, through sales of those assets. But, on the other hand, if your LLC doesn't buy cash-flow positive investments; if the coffee shop fails, those losses will flow back to your pension plan as well.

A white elephant in your early investing days can have some tragic consequences for your pension fund. This is especially important if you are a novice real estate investor and you haven't accounted for all of the hidden costs of ownership (taxes, utilities, maintenance, homeowner association dues, and so forth) in your rental contract. You may wind up renting the property out for less than your overall expenses, creating something that is actually costing you money, instead of making you money.

The same goes for those of you who live in areas with super-heated appreciation rates. If you're investing in those areas, then you already know that sometimes you just can't rent the property out for enough to make it cash-flow neutral, let alone cash-flow positive. These are the properties you're sitting on for a relatively short period of time, eating some of the costs each month, and waiting until the appreciation pushes that property's value high enough that you can sell, recover all of your shortfall, and still walk away with a profit. That's a workable strategy in many instances, but not necessarily something you want to do with your pension funds.

So first and foremost, make sure you have enough money in your pension plan to support the businesses your LLC is going to invest in. Remember—your pension plan funds the LLC—not you. If the business loses money, or if you buy real estate and can't rent it out for enough to cover all of your expenses, the shortfall has to come from somewhere, and that somewhere is your pension plan. Make sure you explore business opportunities thoroughly, and get some input from your plan administrator or other business advisors before getting out the LLC's checkbook.

Another thing to make sure you're aware of is problems with debt leveraging—also called "getting a loan."

Leverage is a wonderful thing—in fact we're going to spend an entire chapter (Chapter 11) explaining how and why debt leverage can move your investments forward at an astonishing pace. But it has some downsides as well—one is the UBIT, and the second is that pension funds have traditionally had a tough time getting loans without first having to come up with a substantial down payment.

If you have enough money in your pension fund to make a down payment, but not enough to purchase a property outright, your LLC is going to need a mortgage. However, because many pension plans are exempt from claims by creditors, if things go south and the LLC defaults on the loan, the lender can't come after your pension—the lender can only chase after any assets held by the LLC. That makes your IRA LLC or Tax-Free LLC a pretty lousy risk from a lender's perspective, which means you're going to be looking at a much higher down payment percentage before your LLC will get a loan. In fact, the typical ratio for pension plan investing is 30/70—you put up 30 percent, and the bank will put up the remaining 70 percent.

WHY THE LLC/PENSION PLAN COMBINATION IS SO EFFECTIVE

We believe that the element of control combined with the ability to leverage pension money into big gains are what makes this strategy so powerful. We've got some examples in Chapter 11 that will show you just how vital leverage is to your overall investing plan. There's also an example on the next couple of pages that shows you the difference between a traditional investment, an IRA LLC investment and a Tax-Free LLC investment.

Could you do most of these things without using an IRA LLC?

Yes, no question. But you probably won't be able to do things as quickly as you can with an IRA LLC, and there may be times where you run into a plan administrator who won't let you make the investments you want to because they conflict with internal company policy.

COMPARISON OF A TRADITIONAL, IRA LLC AND TAX-FREE LLC INVESTMENT

Here's a real-time example of the power of pension investing that demonstrates some of the differences between investing with after-tax money, tax-deferred money, and tax-free money.

Let's assume that you bought a house for $200,000 and sold it two months later, in a typical flip strategy, for a net profit of $100,000. You're already in the 35 percent personal income tax bracket, so you know your profit will be taxed 35 percent. See what happens in each case.

THE TRADITIONAL METHOD

In our first example we've assumed you bought the property with after-tax savings. We've also assumed that:

- You carry on "fix and flips," where you buy properties, fix them up and quickly resell them, typically in less than one year.
- You run your "fix and flip" business through an S Corporation, to maximize the tax advantages and avoid a 15.3 percent self-employment tax (so if you're doing these types of deals in your personal name, consider this your wake-up call).

Your after-tax profit from this deal would be $65,000.

Here's a tip: Because you held the property for less than one year, your profit was considered by the IRS to be ordinary income and taxed the same way your W-2 income would be taxed. If you'd held the property for more than a year you could have taken advantage of the lower capital gains tax rate. If that's the type of investing you plan on doing, an S Corporation won't work to your advantage as much as an LLC would.

Now, let's say you took that $65,000 and continue to invest in other properties. You receive a 10 percent return on your $65,000 investment, and, again, because you've been buying, holding, and selling properties within 1-year periods, you've been paying 35 percent tax on your profits.

Here's what your $65,000 might look like in 5 years	$ 89,883
And again, in 10 years	$124,292

That's not bad, really. Your $65,000 has almost doubled in 10 years. Let's see what happens if we rerun the calculation through an IRA LLC.

THE IRA LLC METHOD

This time, you're starting with deferred-tax money from your IRA LLC. So the first difference is that your initial $100,000 profit isn't subject to tax. Remember, nothing is taxed until you withdraw money from your pension fund. And, because you had more profit at the end of this deal you had more money to work with. We'll assume, though, that you made the same 10 percent return on all of your subsequent investments, and that you pulled everything out of your IRA LLC at the end of 10 years and paid 35 percent in tax.

Here's your total on $100,000 after 10 years	$259,374
Less 35 percent tax to withdraw it all from your IRA	$ (90,781)
Net in your pocket	$168,593

Wow. That $65,000 profit has practically doubled with an IRA LLC plan. Are you curious to see what happens to the same thing in a Tax-Free LLC plan?

THE TAX-FREE LLC METHOD

In this case, you're using money from a Solo Roth 401(k) to invest in the flip. All the details are the same as the preceding two cases, except in this case there is no tax—now or later. However, the money was taxed when you put it into your Solo Roth 401(k) account in the beginning:

Here's your net profit at the end of the first sale	$ 65,000
And here's your tax-free profit at the end of 5 years	$104,683
And here's your tax-free profit at the end of 10 years	$185,453

So—what do you want? $124,000 in 10 years or more than $185,000? Learning about what you can do with your pension money can make a huge difference in how much money you have when you retire.

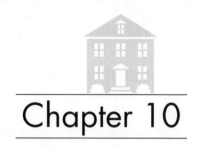

Chapter 10

THE NUTS AND BOLTS OF SETTING UP, MAINTAINING, AND RUNNING YOUR IRA OR TAX-FREE LLC

We hope that the material presented so far has opened your eyes to some of the truly wonderful possibilities that pension investing offers. If you finished Chapter 9 and decided that an IRA LLC or a Tax-Free LLC was the way to go, great! In this chapter, we're going to explore how to get your LLC set up properly, how to keep it set up, and how to carry out some of the daily transactions you'll be required to do.

If you've operated LLCs in the past, then you're probably familiar with many of the basics: appoint a resident agent, prepare and file Articles of Organization with your local state agency, file for a

Tax ID number with the IRS, open a bank account, and prepare an Operating Agreement. But even if you are an experienced LLC owner/operator, bear in mind that the LLCs used to operate with a pension plan are going to be fairly specialized. The Operating Agreement in particular is going to be different, as most plan administrators require special language on several issues, including prohibited transactions. So, even if you are an experienced investor and completely familiar with forming and operating LLCs, you still may not want to form this one on your own. We wouldn't recommend using a corporate formation company that isn't experienced with the intricacies of pension investing, either. If you (or they) do it wrong (and it is easy to do it wrong, if you follow the standard way of doing business), you risk huge penalties with your pension and the possible disqualification of your entire pension.

INSIDE YOUR IRA OR TAX-FREE LLC

As we've already set out, an LLC is a separate, legal business structure that functions completely independently of its owners, the same way that a corporation does. (You may own Wal-Mart stock, but you certainly don't have a hot line to the president.) An IRA or Tax-Free LLC will have two levels: a member/owner, which is your pension plan, and a manager, which is you personally. Your pension fund will own 100 percent of the LLC's membership interests, which are the equivalent of a corporation's shares.

> LLCs are considered separate legal entities. That means owners can't be sued. The most your pension fund could lose is whatever it has invested in the LLC.

WHAT IT TAKES TO FORM AN IRA LLC
OR TAX-FREE LLC

The steps to set up an LLC are fairly straightforward. You need to:

1. Decide on the state you'll form your LLC in.
2. Find a resident agent (you can act as your own resident agent but you may not always want to).
3. Prepare and file your LLC's articles.
4. Once the Articles come back, prepare the post-formation documents including an Operating Agreement with specialized pension-related language.
5. File for a Tax ID number with the IRS.
6. Make any secondary filings that your state requires.

WHERE SHOULD YOUR IRA LLC OR TAX-FREE LLC
BE FORMED

With traditional LLCs, where you form the structure depends on a few things, like the location of your business operations or real estate property or properties and any taxation issues that may arise as a result of its location. But because taxation isn't an issue to your IRA LLC or Tax-Free LLC, you don't really have much to consider here.

It's usually easiest to form your LLC in the state where the assets it will be holding are located. If your LLC owns assets in multiple states, it may need to register to do business in each state, at least for so long as the LLC owns those assets.

But because your LLC will be paying filing and maintenance fees in each state, this often brings up the question of what happens if you don't register your IRA or Tax-Free LLC in each state where it holds assets.

The answer is "it depends." Many states are vague on what they consider "doing business" in that state, and when a foreign entity (which in this context means any entity not formed in that state) is required to register. The basic rule of "Do you make money here? Then you owe money here," doesn't always apply. In fact, you'll hear all sorts of things, from "owns or rents property," to "engages independent contractors to carry out business on its behalf" (ouch!). In most states the passive ownership of bare land is enough to constitute "doing business."

However, the most compelling reason to register your IRA or Tax-Free LLC in each state where you do business is because you may not be able to bring suit in that state if you don't. So, let's say some tenants decided not to pay the rent and, before you could evict them, trashed the property they were renting from your IRA or Tax-Free LLC. If your IRA or Tax-Free LLC is properly registered to do business in that state you can sue those tenants for back rent and damages. But if the LLC isn't registered, you may not be able to sue those tenants at all.

Steve and Eva live in California and invest in other states. They are now exploring using their self-directed IRA to invest in a property in Arizona. They understand the practical need of having an LLC to operate the day-to-day operation and so want to set one up. They also know that the IRA LLC is not the same as a plain off-the-shelf LLC and so understand it'll probably take a little extra time to get it set up.

The question is, in what state should they form the LLC? Since the LLC will be holding property in Arizona, the LLC would be formed in Arizona. If Steve and Eva later decide to buy property in California, it probably would make the most sense for them to form another LLC in California for that separate property. However, if they buy a second property in Arizona, they can continue to use the same Arizona LLC.

FIND A RESIDENT AGENT FOR YOUR IRA OR TAX-FREE LLC

A resident agent (sometimes also called a "statutory" agent or a "registered" agent) is your LLC's legal face in each state where your IRA or Tax-Free LLC is doing business. The primary purpose of a resident agent is to accept service of legal documents on behalf of your LLC. That's why resident agents are required in almost every state. Without a resident agent, your business doesn't have proper legal standing to operate in that state.

Your LLC Players

Manager—You (responsible for self-directing your LLC's investments on behalf of your pension fund).

Member—Your pension fund (owns your LLC and funds its operations).

Custodian—An unrelated third party that holds your pension's assets and helps you to comply with IRS regulations for investments.

Resident Agent—You or (preferably) an unrelated third party that acts as your LLC's legal representative and address for all service of legal documents.

There are two exceptions to the resident agent requirement: New York and West Virginia. But even in these two states you are still required to designate an address as your resident agent (in this case the attorney general's office), and authorize that office to accept service on behalf of your IRA or Tax-Free LLC.

There are resident agent companies available in every state. You can expect to pay a yearly fee for this service. Resident agents may also offer additional services, such as providing you with a mailing address in that state and forwarding mail to you. Your resident agent should also make sure that any annual state filings are done on behalf of your LLC and may also offer an annual minutes service. We've provided some suggestions for resident agent service at our web site, www.reirallc.com.

A CAUTION ON ACTING AS YOUR OWN RESIDENT AGENT

Many people try to save money by acting personally as the resident agent for their IRA or Tax-Free LLC. You can do this—there is no conflict with your also acting as the manager. But remember—a resident agent accepts service of legal documents. That means a resident agent needs to be available during regular business hours, and that your personal address will be a part of the public record. So, if you are a frequent traveler, being your own resident agent may not be the best idea, as it could restrict your movements. You may also not necessarily want to make yourself so readily available to potential litigants, either. Once you are served with a legal document, you have a set period of time in which to file a reply, or you risk losing the argument by default, simply because you didn't file a response on time.

PREPARE AND FILE YOUR IRA LLC OR TAX-FREE LLC ARTICLES

You can expect to fill out a form that will run between one and three pages, and then to file that report with the Secretary of State's office (or the Division of Corporations, Department of State, and so forth), along with the appropriate fee. The actual information you'll be writing down on each form will differ

John owned several properties in the Las Vegas area. To minimize his risk, he held each property in a separate LLC. This meant he had four LLCs in total. As he lived in Phoenix, John had to appoint a resident agent company to accept service of process for each of the LLCs. That meant paying four separate resident agent fees, and John thought this was a waste of money. One year John decided to name himself as resident agent and use one of his properties as his registered address in Nevada. He asked his tenant (Tenant 1) to forward all mail that was addressed to him personally or to any of his LLCs.

Everything appeared to be fine, right up until the time John got into a dispute with Tenant 1. While he and Tenant 1 were feuding, however, another tenant (Tenant 2) was having a wild house party that got out of control. A young girl was assaulted, and her parents sued both Tenant 2, as the party's host, and John, as the owner of the property.

When the process server arrived at the door of Tenant 1 he had no problem serving the documents—Tenant 1 signed the paperwork with no comment. But that was as far as it went. Tenant 1 then pitched the lawsuit into a trashcan by the door, along with the rest of John's LLC-related mail. John was never notified of the lawsuit against him until a sheriff came knocking at his door in Phoenix, looking to collect on the damages awarded to the young woman at Tenant 2's party. John had no chance to defend himself, and was left trying to fend off his creditors while trying to have the original order set aside. In hindsight, John figured that those resident agent service fees seemed a small cost when compared with this alternative.

from state to state, but you can expect to at least provide the following:

- Name.
- Business Address (this can be a PO Box).
- Resident Agent name and street address.

- Selection of manager or member-managed.
- Name and mailing address of all managers (if your LLC is manager-managed).
- Signature of at least one organizer (the person or business submitting the Articles).
- Signature (or separate consent form) of your resident agent, consenting to their appointment.

More and more states are adopting an online filing system for business structures that allows you to submit and pay for a formation without leaving your computer. The articles are processed at the Secretary of State's office electronically and the file-stamped articles can be downloaded either on the spot or within a day or two. This is much faster than mailing in the paperwork, and that can be a huge advantage, especially if you're trying to get your IRA LLC or Tax-Free LLC set up quickly. Other states offer a priority filing service, but that will cost more.

PREPARING THE POST-FORMATION PAPERWORK

The document that defines how an LLC is to be structured and operated is called an Operating Agreement. This document sets out the following key points (in addition to other administrative functions):

- Whether the LLC is member-managed, manager-managed, or managed by a select group of members.
- Whether the LLC chooses to use traditional management titles such as President, Secretary, and so forth.
- How managers or managing members are appointed or removed.

- Restrictions on ownership and transfer of membership interests.
- How the profits and losses are to be distributed among the members.
- What happens in the event of the LLC's bankruptcy.
- The circumstances under which a member may be bought out by other members.
- How disputes between managers, members, or both are resolved.
- The level of control managers have over day-to-day operations of the LLC, and when management actions will require preapproval by the members.
- How the Operating Agreement may be changed.
- How members may leave and join the LLC.
- When an LLC may ask its members for additional cash or property contributions, and what happens when members cannot or refuse to pay.

The Operating Agreement is crucial to any LLC's smooth operation. Without it, your LLC is left at the mercy of state laws, which may not allow you to do the things that you had planned.

For an IRA LLC or a Tax-Free LLC, this document is even more essential. Many of the points set out above must be modified or removed entirely—for example, an IRA LLC or a Tax-Free LLC must be manager-managed only—you can't operate it as a member-managed structure and still have it work with your pension fund. You will need specially worded sections on asking for additional cash or property contributions and how members may transfer ownership. And you'll also need some entirely new sections dealing with the following:

- Prohibited transactions.
- Disqualified persons.

- Duties and responsibilities of both the Manager and the Plan Administrator.
- Listed transactions that are subject to IRS Notice 2004-8.
- Acknowledgment of the impact of the *Rollins* case.

Your plan administrator will want to review and approve your LLC's Operating Agreement before you can proceed to set up your IRA or Tax-Free LLC.

Given all of the above, this is one area where you really don't want to go it alone. You probably won't find an off-the-shelf Operating Agreement available through formation services or from web sites that will cover the IRA LLC or the Tax-Free LLC. In the long run, this is probably something best left to your attorney or a formation service that is experienced in this type of business structure.*

APPLYING FOR A TAX ID NUMBER FROM THE IRS

Every business formed in the United States is required by law to have an Employer Identification Number (also called a Tax ID number). This number serves the same purpose for your IRA or Tax-Free LLC as your social security number does for you personally. It provides the government with a way to identify your LLC for tax purposes and will be required before you can open up bank accounts in the name of your business structure or obtain a business license, insurance, open vendor accounts, and so forth.

If you file for your IRA or Tax-Free LLC's Tax ID number online, make sure to write down the provisional Tax ID number

---

*To find service providers who offer the IRA LLC and Tax-Free LLC formation and maintenance, see our Rolodex at www.reirallc.com.

that will be displayed on your computer screen once your application has been accepted, and then print that page as well. If you don't, and your printer jams, or you lose the number, it will take up to one week before the IRS staff can access that number in their database.

Fortunately, the IRS has made getting your LLC's Tax ID number very easy. The application form, called a Form SS-4, can be preprinted on your computer and mailed or faxed in to the IRS (the most time-consuming method), or you can apply over the telephone and receive your number faster. You can also apply online and receive a Tax ID number instantly. The link to this portion of the IRS's web site is https://sa.www4.irs.gov/sa_vign/newFormSS4.do.

SECONDARY FILINGS

The last set-up item you may need to take care of is a secondary filing to accompany your LLC's Articles of Organization. This usually takes the form of some type of report. For example in California it's called a Statement of Information, while in Nevada it's called the Initial List. Not all states have this secondary filing requirement, but if your state does and you don't make this filing your LLC can be penalized or even administratively dissolved by the state.

ANNUAL FILINGS

Many states have an annual filing requirement. This is going to be very similar to the secondary filing we discussed above. There is usually a fee to file this document.

If you are using a third-party resident agent service, you should be notified by your agent of any annual filing requirements and the costs. If you're acting as your own resident agent, keep an eye on this. Again, if you forget to do your IRA or Tax-Free LLC's annual filings, you could wind up having to pay a financial penalty or having your LLC dissolved.

If your LLC is dissolved for failure to file, it can usually be recovered, although again, this will cost money. It can also be very problematic from a legal standpoint, as it can cloud ownership of all of its assets. Think about it—if your IRA LLC holds title to a rental property, and the entity no longer exists legally, then who (or what) owns that property?

HOW YOUR IRA LLC OR TAX-FREE LLC IS TAXED

Most LLCs don't pay taxes. In fact, if you were to go to the IRS's web site you wouldn't be able to find an LLC tax return form. That's because an LLC can choose how it wants to be taxed—as a partnership, as a corporation, or as something called a "single member disregarded" entity. If your LLC is taxed as a corporation (either a C or an S Corporation), it would maintain its books the same way a corporation would and would file the same type of tax return as the corporation it was emulating (Form 1120 for a C Corporation and Form 1120S for an S Corporation). If your LLC was being taxed as a partnership, it would keep its books like a partnership and prepare a partnership return (Form 1065). If your LLC was being taxed as a single-member disregarded, it wouldn't necessarily need to keep separate books at all, and you would simply prepare a Schedule C to go along with your regular personal tax return.

For the purposes of your IRA LLC or Tax-Free LLC, though, the partnership taxation route is best. That means the LLC will keep its own business records, and will flow all of its net profit (or loss) through to your pension fund. The tax form that records the profit distribution is called a Schedule K-1, and it is prepared by the LLC at the same time the Form 1065 is prepared. If you've got an IRA LLC, any taxes owing will be deferred until you begin making withdrawals from your pension. If you've got a Tax-Free LLC, then your pension fund is a tax-free plan, meaning that none of the LLC's income will be taxed (unless you're using a Roth IRA and have UBIT to worry about).

WHEN YOUR IRA LLC OR TAX-FREE LLC CAN DISTRIBUTE PROFITS

Your LLC can distribute profits through the year, or at the end of the year after the taxes are done. This is done by issuing a check, made payable to your plan's custodian or administrator, for the benefit of your pension fund. Your administrator can tell you exactly how the checks should be worded. Each time a profit distribution is made, the LLC's bookkeeper will make an entry in the books noting the distribution, and at the end of the year these amounts will be noted on the Schedule K-1.

CAN YOUR IRA LLC OR TAX-FREE LLC PAY YOU A SALARY?

In a normal LLC, members never receive a salary, although the managers usually do. But this is one of the key differences between a standard LLC and an IRA or Tax-Free LLC—managers *cannot* receive a salary. That's because you can't receive any direct benefits from your pension. If you were to be paid a salary for managing your own LLC in this case, you would be directly benefiting from the income earned by your pension fund. So while you're contributing your management services for free, just keep in mind how much value you're adding to your overall pension at the end of the day.

CAN YOUR IRA LLC OR TAX-FREE LLC REIMBURSE YOU FOR EXPENSES?

Yes! If you have legitimate expenses in carrying out the business of the LLC, you can be reimbursed for them. That's not the same as benefiting from your pension's profits. But make sure you have good records and receipts for all expenses you are claiming.

PERSONAL LIABILITY AND YOUR IRA LLC OR YOUR TAX-FREE LLC

One question that comes up frequently from people considering this strategy is that, by acting as the LLC's manager, does he or she become personally liable for any debts of the IRA or Tax-Free LLC.

The answer is usually no. An LLC is considered by law to be a separate legal entity. That means the members are not liable for the acts or debts of the LLC, and cannot be sued or lose anything other than the money or assets they had previously contributed to the LLC. That same protection also applies to the manager. The only time a court may find the manager of an LLC personally liable for an action or debt of an LLC is if it is proven to the court that a manager was using the LLC to carry out illegal actions, or was using the LLC to benefit himself or herself personally and not acting in the best interests of the LLC and its members.

THE SPECIAL ASSET PROTECTION LLCS ENJOY

Most states subscribe to a special asset protection treatment that allows the owners of LLCs to keep the assets held in the name of the LLC intact when the owners are personally sued.

For example, let's say you injure someone in a car accident, and wind up being sued. You are found at fault, and the injured person is awarded damages against you in the amount of $100,000. If you can't write a check to the injured person for that amount, that person has the right to take certain of your assets, up to the $100,000 you owe.

Even if you don't have enough money to pay that $100,000, if you have an LLC that owns real estate worth $500,000, your LLC and its real estate assets are both safe from that injured person. That's because the special asset protection doesn't allow the injured person to reach into your LLC.

But what it does allow the injured person to do is to place something called a "Charging Order" over all of the assets in the LLC. A Charging Order works like a garnishing order—any profits made by the LLC are diverted away from you to the injured person, until your debt has been paid in full. And while this isn't great for you or your pension, it certainly beats the alternative—having your pension's assets taken away and sold.

> A Charging Order will protect your LLC's assets from your personal actions, misdeeds and debts.
>
> A Charging Order won't protect your LLC from its own actions, misdeeds or debts.

It's important to note here that this special asset protection doesn't apply to your IRA LLC or Tax-Free LLC itself. If your LLC is operating a coffee shop that can't pay its bills, or if someone is injured on a property owned by your LLC, and your property insurance doesn't cover the damages, then the assets in the LLC are at risk. But a creditor can't reach through the LLC into your pension.

Actually, this brings up an important point: If you're planning to own lots of real estate or businesses, you may want to use more than one IRA LLC or Tax-Free LLC. There is no limit to the number of LLCs your pension can own, and it would be a good way to keep your assets protected. If you owned two pieces of real estate as well as that coffee shop, it might be better to put the coffee shop into a separate IRA LLC. That way, if it couldn't pay its bills and went out of business, any creditors looking to be paid would have to be satisfied with whatever assets they could liquidate from the coffee shop—they could not reach out to your other real estate investments.

DOING BUSINESS IN THE NAME OF YOUR IRA LLC OR TAX-FREE LLC

As you begin to self-direct your pension investments, it is important to always do business in the name of your IRA or Tax-Free LLC.* That means make sure that you sign all contracts between your LLC and another person or company in your official capacity. So, you would always sign as "John Doe, Manager, ABC LLC, instead of just "John Doe." That includes everything from an in-store credit card application at Office Depot to mortgage documentation. There are two reasons for this. First, you don't want to wind up stuck in a self-dealing situation because you signed something personally. Second, when you sign things personally and don't make it clear that you are signing in an official capacity, you can be held personally liable for whatever contract you just entered into.

---

*Diane offers a publication specifically designed for LLC owners that goes through all of the steps to plan, set up, operate and maintain your LLC. To learn more visit her web site at www.taxloopholes.com and look for the Operation Guide for Your LLC or LP.

RECORD KEEPING REQUIREMENTS FOR YOUR IRA LLC OR TAX-FREE LLC

Record-keeping is another important step. If you want to self-direct your investments, then you *must* keep excellent records of all money coming in and out of your IRA or Tax-Free LLC. Remember, you must live up to the expectations of both your plan administrator *and* the IRS.

Keeping your formation documents is the easier of the two steps. Many people order a professional Minute Book binder, which usually contains section tabs, a seal, Interest Certificates, and blank minute paper. You can order Minute Books online from various sources and, generally speaking, you can expect to pay between $50 and $100. However, you can also accomplish the same thing with a simple three-ring binder from Walgreen's. Company seals are nice to have, but not essential, as they are no longer required to be used on contracts in U.S. law (or in most other countries). Blank Interest Certificates and minute paper can be purchased from any stationery store. The point is, keep the records up to date and preferably in a single location.

Other business records, like contracts, property deeds, bills of sale for equipment and warranty information, and so forth, don't have to be kept in the Minute Book, but should be kept in a file folder or other secure location. These records should be kept with your current financial and daily business records until the contracts are completed or cancelled, and then removed to storage with that year's business financial records. If you're ever in doubt, ask your plan administrator what records you need to keep, or if there are any records that your plan administrator needs to keep, and make sure to follow the instructions you're given.

SECTION FIVE

Tricks and Traps of Leverage

Chapter 11

LEVERAGING YOUR MONEY

Leverage multiplies force to accomplish large tasks with small resources. A long plank placed atop a small fulcrum can move a boulder. When the Egyptians built the great pyramid at Giza, three men using levers moved blocks of stone weighing more than two and a half tons. Almost no one can pull a nail from a wall with a bare hand. By using the claw on a hammer, that same hand can easily pull out a nail.

Leverage in financial matters works the same way by using the cash you have to get a much greater financial impact. If you buy a property for $100,000 and rent it for $10,000 per year, you will get a 10 percent return (the $10,000 rental divided by the $100,000 purchase price). However, if you get a mortgage for 50 percent of the purchase price at say 6 percent interest (costing you $3,000 a year in interest if the loan were interest-only) you would end up with $7,000 net on a $50,000 investment, or 14 percent return. Similarly, a 90 percent mortgage would leave you with $4,600 net on $10,000 investment, or 46 percent return. And if you managed to finance the entire purchase price of $100,000, you would still collect $4,000 net of mortgage interest, but in this case, with no capital tied up, you would have an infinite rate of return. Leverage, or using a mortgage, can greatly increase your cash-on-cash return.

Now we know many of you will be thinking, "Right, how am I supposed to get a mortgage for 100 percent of the purchase price?" Well, one of the great things about real estate is that this sort of financing is not only possible, but easy. While it is true that most banks prefer to see a 10 percent, or for investors even a 20 percent down payment, banks do lend 90 percent of the purchase price, 95 percent, or even 100 percent. In fact it is possible to get mortgages of 125 percent at present.

However, should you have no success negotiating such a mortgage, there are many other ways of achieving 100 percent financing. For instance, there is nothing to stop you getting a first mortgage for 80 percent of the purchase price, and a second mortgage for the remaining 20 percent. The interest rate on the second mortgage may be a bit higher (to reflect the higher risk taken by the bank on the grounds that if you fall behind in your payments, the first mortgage gets paid off in full before the second mortgage holder gets anything). There are even banks and lending institutions that offer a so-called 80-20 combination loan.

Or when you put in an offer to buy a property, you could ask the seller to leave in some money in the form of a note. Such a loan is often referred to as a seller carry-back. For instance, if you got the seller to agree to leaving in 30 percent at say 6 percent interest, and you also managed to get a first mortgage for 80 percent, then you will even have money left over.

Another option when you buy a property is to ask for the closing to take place in two or three months' time with the right of access to the property in the interim to effect improvements. Then, when you are about to close, you get a new appraisal, which will reflect the higher, improved value. An 80 percent loan based on the new improved value may well be more than the entire original purchase price.

In reality, when you suggest 100 percent financing to most people, they think you must be on drugs or something, because the notion of acquiring real estate without putting up any cash is outside their comfort zone. However, the more you get involved in real estate, the more you will realize that not only is it possible to obtain 100 percent financing, but it can be obtained relatively easily. Sometimes, all you have to do is politely ask a seller if he would consider leaving some money in. You will be surprised at how often the seller says yes.

While we have discussed the benefits of leverage on a relatively small scale, leverage also works for much larger projects. A developer building a $40 million resort will probably not have $40 million in cash to fund the development. However, depending on his track record, presales, and the merits of the project, he may be able to obtain seed capital and a development loan from financial institutions. In this case, the leverage simply enables him to do a deal he otherwise wouldn't be able to do without financial institutions.

Using leverage for any investment can greatly improve cash on cash returns, and can enable deals to occur that would not happen without the leverage. The great thing about real estate is that banks and other financial institutions are very keen to lend money using your real estate as collateral for the loan. Evidence of this are the scores of billboards, newspaper advertisements, television advertisements, and spam e-mails offering money in the form of mortgages. You do not see ads saying things like, "Want to buy gold, diamonds, baseball cards, phone cards, stocks, bonds, certificates of deposit, treasury bills, or mutual funds? Come and see us! We will give you a competitive interest rate! We even have mobile loan officers who will see you at a time and place to suit you!" Banks do not like to lend money against these items. But when it comes to real estate, they are competing against each other.

Leverage gives you tremendous power when you invest. Real estate is the vehicle that banks want you to leverage. It is a powerful and fortuitous combination.

Chapter 12

THE CONSEQUENCES OF LEVERAGING

Leverage will grow your wealth faster. But there can be some tax consequences to using leverage with your pension plan. We'll look at those issues and provide some strategies to reduce the negative affect of the investments.

There are two challenges to using leverage with your IRA or Solo 401(k) plans. The two issues are:

1. Getting a loan without running into a prohibited transaction.
2. Avoiding UDFI (Unrelated Debt-Financed Income Tax).

Let's talk about the first issue—getting a loan without running into a prohibited transaction.

Getting a loan can take a few extra steps when you're working with a pension. The problem is that you cannot personally guarantee the loan if your pension is investing in the deal. If you do guarantee the loan, either directly or because you have a "recourse" loan, then you have a prohibited transaction. Remember, having a prohibited transaction means your entire IRA account may become immediately subject to tax and penalties.

There are now a couple of banks that will make nonrecourse loans directly to pension plans. As we mentioned in an earlier chapter though, these banks require a 70 percent or less loan to value ratio. For example, let's say you find a duplex (a two-family home) that you want to buy for $300,000. Your IRA can buy the property with a loan for 70 percent of the value, which means your IRA would provide $90,000 for the down payment and closing costs, and take out a loan for the remaining $210,000 of the purchase price.

One word of warning: do not completely tap out your IRA fund when you buy the property. There may be added expenses or some cash flow down turns due to maintenance or vacancies, and it's difficult to put more money into the deal. Make sure you have enough to start with. Also, you'll need to perform due diligence in conjunction with your lender and make sure your lender's given you a pretty strong thumbs up on the loan before you commit nonrefundable IRA LLC money or have your pension administrator commit nonrefundable pension money on the deal.

This might be a good time to review the do's and don'ts of buying property with your pension. You can't deal directly with your pension. That means your pension plan can't buy, sell, or rent a property to or from you. You also can't put money down on a property from your personal account (even in a refundable deposit) and then have your pension involved in the deal. If any of your personal money touches the deal, it's tainted for your pension. By the same token, you personally cannot get a loan for a property if your pension has any money in the deal.

WHAT IF YOUR PENSION PLAN DOESN'T HAVE ENOUGH MONEY?

Here's something that probably will come up for most people, at least in the early days—your pension plan doesn't have the full 30 percent needed to qualify for a 70 percent nonrecourse loan. What can you do?

Just about anything you want, actually. Here are some suggestions, if you find yourself in this predicament:

- Do you have multiple small pension plans that you've resisted rolling over, or just haven't gotten around to rolling over yet? You can combine all of those amounts as long as they are all self-directed plans that allow you to purchase real estate.
- If you have enough cash in savings, you can invest both your pension funds and your personal funds, as long as you make sure the property is being held as Tenants-in-Common. This creates a separate legal relationship over each portion of the property (50:50, 60:40, 75:25, and so forth) and does not create a prohibited transaction. If someone dies, his ownership percentage passes to his heirs, rather than being divided among the remaining owners. It's really as though you each own separate properties in that respect. So if you die, your part of the property would go to your heirs, while the portion owned by your pension would go to its beneficiaries.
- The same Tenants-in-Common method works for friends and other family members as well. So if you have a brother or sister who wants to go in on the deal they can—and so can their pensions.
- You could even use this method to get around the problems with debt inside pensions that we'll discuss below. Rather than having your pension incur the debt, another person who is part of the deal could borrow the money instead.

157

- If you don't want to involve anyone else, you could make things work by taking out an equity loan against your own home or any other properties you own that aren't inside your pension. Now you can use the proceeds from that loan to finance the purchase of the new property. In this case you are putting your home up as collateral, which means you can get away from nonrecourse financing limits.
- Something to remember with any type of multiperson or business financing is that you must split your profits and expenses strictly according to your ownership percentages. So if you take out a home loan to purchase a property and have a 30 percent interest in the property, you can't sell the property and give yourself 35 percent of the profits to compensate you for taking on the loan in the first place. That turns the transaction into a prohibited transaction.

Please note that you need to run the above ideas by your tax advisor or plan custodian before you put them in place. In some cases, the disqualified person rule can come into play and you may not be able to qualify for one of or more of these strategies. If you're concerned about a possible prohibited transaction, consider rolling the amount that you will invest in the project into a separate IRA. In other words, if you have $50,000 in a plan and want to invest $20,000 in a strategy that might fall into the gray area, roll the $20,000 into a separate IRA. That way, if you do end up in trouble with the plan, the worst that will happen is that the $20,000 will become immediately taxable.

USING AN LLC

Throughout the rest of this chapter, we'll be talking about pension investing through either an IRA LLC or a Tax-Free LLC. Having the LLC involved doesn't change the law or tax issues. We recommend the LLC/pension plan combination method simply because it makes the administration so much easier, and that means it's much easier for you and your plan custodian to make sure you're in compliance with the sometimes cumbersome pension investing requirements.

UDFI (UNRELATED DEBT-FINANCED INCOME TAX)

The one downside of leverage in an IRA LLC is something called UDFI (unrelated debt-financed income tax).

First, let's start with some background on what UDFI actually is. In the 1950s, the IRS Code was amended to include a provision called unrelated business taxable income or UBTI. This became Code Section 514. The tax on this income is called unrelated business income tax (UBIT).

If a nonprofit business engages in a business that is unrelated to its primary purpose, the income from the business is subject to UBIT. So if you operate a nonprofit food bank, and your food bank workers also design and sell web sites, your food bank will pay UBIT on the income it earns from the web site design and sales.

In addition to UBIT, whenever debt is used by a tax-deferred or tax-exempt entity (with some exceptions) to earn income, another tax is also calculated and assessed. This tax is called unrelated debt financing income tax (UDFI), and it's this tax that is assessed on a pension that holds leveraged property.

CALCULATING UDFI

The first step in calculating UDFI is to calculate the "acquisition indebtedness." Acquisition indebtedness is the outstanding amount of principal debt incurred by a pension to either acquire or improve the property in one of two methods:

1. Before the property was acquired or improved, if the debt was incurred because of the acquisition or improvement of the property.
2. After the property was acquired or improved, if the debt was incurred because of the acquisition or improvement, and the organization could reasonably foresee the need to incur the debt at the time the property was acquired or improved.

Now, the *average* indebtedness for the property is determined. Let's assume that (based on the acquisition price) at the beginning of the year, the property has 70 percent acquisition indebtedness. At the end of the year, this has been reduced to 68 percent. Average the indebtedness, and you find that it is 69 percent for the year. If you ended up selling the property at the end of the year and made $100,000 in profit, then 69 percent (or $69,000) of the gain would be subject to UDFI.

If you held a property for a long-term investment as a rental, you'd also owe tax on the net rental income represented by the debt-financed portion. The taxable income from the property can be offset by depreciation, but the depreciation must be calculated using the straight-line method. Other expenses, prorated to reflect the average indebtedness, can be used to offset the income prior to the tax being calculated.

IRS Publication 598 lays out the detail for the rules on debt-financed property and income tax, if you'd like to try the do-it-yourself approach for the calculation. Our suggestion is that you instead become familiar with the basic rules and then find a qualified advisor to help you with the nuts and bolts of putting together a strategy that includes UDFI.

Does the possibility of UDFI mean that you should avoid leverage in your pension plan? Let's look at a couple of exam-

Kathy's first IRA LLC property was a rental property. At some point, she may end up selling it, but her initial thought was to hold the property for a while. Kathy bought the property with 50 percent down and took out an interest-only mortgage for the remaining 50 percent.

She rented the property for a positive cash flow of $200 per month. Kathy's taxable income (cash basis) was the same because all of the property-related expenses were completely deductible. That meant Kathy had taxable income of $2,400 per year, 50 percent of which would be subject to UDFI. But, Kathy first got to take a deduction for depreciation. Because 50 percent of the property was subject to UDFI, 50 percent of the basis was also subject to depreciation. In this case, the depreciation deduction completely wiped out the UDFI taxable income.

ples to see what happens when you use leverage and when you don't.

AVOIDING UDFI

Is it possible to avoid UDFI? Yes! In fact, we've got two possible methods to do it.

First, consider how UDFI is actually calculated. It is a calculation based on the average indebtedness compared to the total property price (creating a percentage) applied to the income from the property.

There are two primary ways that you can make money from your real estate. One way is through the rental income you will make from rental properties. The rental income will be offset by a pro-rata share of expenses related to the property and a pro-rata share of straight line depreciation calculated on the property.

Straight line depreciation is one method of calculating depreciation. Generally, property purchased through more traditional means use MACRS (modified accelerated cost recovery system) calculations for depreciation.

In general, if you're taking advantage of all of the expenses that you can for your real estate, you'll be showing very little, if any, taxable gain during the time you're holding the property. So, you probably won't have an UDFI issue during the long-term hold period.

The UDFI issue generally comes up when you sell the property—the second way you can make money on real estate held in your pension. In this case, you have capital gains income and that means some taxable income. But remember, the calculation for UDFI is based on average indebtedness for the past 12 months, applied to the income. So, if you've got cash in your pension, you have another option. Pay off the mortgage on your pension's property at least 12 months prior to the date of sale and you'll completely avoid the UDFI issue. That's probably the simplest solution, especially if you have the cash in your pension.

But the best solution to avoiding UDFI on leveraged property is the second solution—use a Solo 401(k) or a Solo Roth 401(k) plan. Section 514 of the IRS Code says that a 401(k) plan is exempt from paying UDFI. A normal 401(k) plan cannot take advantage of this, because it can't self-direct funds. But the new Solo 401(k) and Solo Roth 401(k)* plans can self-direct their funds. That means you can completely avoid UDFI!

---

*To review the latest requirements to set up a Solo Roth 401(k), please visit our web site at www.reirallc.com. Remember these important tax updates are free, and we would never sell, rent, or otherwise misuse your e-mail address when you contact us.

COMPARE INVESTMENTS IN A TAX-DEFERRED AND A TAX-FREE PENSION

It may seem that it doesn't make sense to buy property within a pension plan if you're going to leverage. In fact, some people think that the only way to proceed is if you can pay cash. Otherwise, UDFI might just eat up your profits. But, is that true? Let's look at what happens if you have to pay UDFI on a property, using a real-life example.

PLAN A: FLIPPING WITH AFTER-TAX DOLLARS

The following is a real life example. The folks in this case did their deal with after-tax dollars and paid the regular tax on it. We'll go through other variations of the same deal in Plan B and Plan C. But first let's look at what actually happened.

"We bought our first home for the princely sum of $82,000. It was a bit run-down, and we thought we could double our money in a few weeks. Of course the reality is far removed from that. It turned out to be a lot more than 'a bit run down.' We had to replace some pilings, replace most of the roof, do some structural work, remodel the kitchen, replace one bathroom, and so on and so forth. Total cost of the work was $46,000. We sold it for $153,000. Not a bad profit, but for 6 months of work, not great either.

"We learned from this, and our next property was in a much better condition, and still only $95,500. This time we spent only $18,000 and 11 weeks, and sold it for $149,000—less than the first one, but the profits were larger and faster.

"Our third flip was acquired for $109,000, we spent $22,000, and sold it for $161,000. Each time we learned new short-cuts, found supplies at better prices, and got better and better contractors. There is still a lot of time involved to get the job done, however. And it sure beats working for a living!"—*John and Sandra, Redding, CA*

The Tax Calculation

John and Sandra were real estate "flippers" who unfortunately didn't consult with a CPA ahead of time. They did the flips in their own names, which mean they had a lot of risk plus they paid the highest amount of tax possible. Luckily, no one has sued, so they were okay with the risk, but the tax due was an unpleasant surprise.

	Tax Due
Home #1 The total gain was $25,000. John and Sandra owed 15.3 percent in self-employment tax, plus 35 percent in federal tax. (They also owed state tax, living in California, but in this case we're just going to take federal taxes into account.)	$12,575
Home #2 The total gain was $35,500. Again, John and Sandra had to pay self-employment and federal tax on their profits (as well as state tax).	$17,856
Home #3 The total gain was $30,000. Again, John and Sandra had to pay self-employment and federal tax on their profits (as well as state tax).	$15,090
Total Taxes Paid by John and Sandra:	$45,521
Total Gain Made by John and Sandra	$44,978

When it was all said and done, John and Sandra could put $44,978—almost $45,000—in their pockets. Not bad!

Now let's take that out a few years. At a modest 10 percent return (which after a maximum federal tax rate of 35 percent taxes equates to 6.5 percent), that $45,000 would be worth:

John and Sandra's After-Tax Investment

Investment Term	Earnings (Rounded to Nearest 1,000)
5 Years	$ 62,000
10 Years	$ 84,000
15 Years	$116,000
20 years	$159,000

Well, not quite enough to retire on, but it's a good start! Now let's look at Plan B to see how they could have done it with pension plans.

Plan B: John and Sandra Take Wealth Building Up a Notch with a Tax-Deferred Plan!

What if they had used an IRA (SEP, Rollover, Contributory or other) for the property? The IRA LLC 5-Step Leverage Plan would be to

1. Roll their current pensions into a self-directed plan, using one of our recommended custodians.
2. Form an IRA LLC to handle the administration. The LLC can then write the checks directly for the fix-up and maintenance of the properties.*
3. Get a loan for the property. We'll assume that John and Sandra had enough funds in their IRAs for the down payment and fix-up money.
4. Sell the property.
5. Pay the taxes due to UDFI.

---

*Remember that an IRA LLC is set up differently from a regular LLC. We strongly recommend that you use one of our experienced referrals for this process. See www.reirallc.com for referrals.

	Tax Due
Home #1 The total gain was $25,000. The UDFI tax would be due on the leveraged portion. We'll assume that they had a 70 percent loan-to-value nonrecourse loan.	$6,125
Home #2 The total gain was $35,500. Again, we'll assume that there is a nonrecourse loan for 70 percent of the property's value and that UDFI is due on that portion.	$8,697
Home #3 The total gain was $30,000. Again, we'll assume that there is a nonrecourse loan for 70 percent of the property's value and that UDFI is due on that portion.	$7,350
Total Taxes Paid by John and Sandra:	$22,172
Total Gain Made by John and Sandra	$68,328

When it was all said and done, John and Sandra made $68,000, instead of $45,000 from Plan A (after tax money). There will be some tax due when they withdraw the proceeds, though. Let's follow the calculation through and assume they made 10 percent on their money during the time they held the money. In this case, the 10 percent would not be immediately taxed, unlike the tax that is due on the after-tax plan.

Now let's take that out a few years. At a modest 10 percent return, that $68,000 would be worth:

Investment Term	Earnings	Tax Due (Rounded)	Net
5 Years	$110,000	$ 17,000	$ 93,000
10 Years	$176,000	$ 43,000	$133,000
15 Years	$284,000	$ 84,000	$200,000
20 Years	$475,000	$153,000	$322,000

Let's compare using the IRA LLC strategy with Plan A, the real-life plan that John and Sandra had used:

166

Investment Term	Plan B IRA LLC (Net)	Plan A After-Tax (Net)
5 Years	$ 95,000	$ 62,000
10 Years	$138,000	$ 84,000
15 Years	$208,000	$116,000
20 Years	$321,000	$159,000

Which would you choose? Investing with a tax-deferred IRA might be more work, but over time, there can be huge benefits.

Now let's look at investing with the truly tax-free plan—the Tax-Free LLC combined with the Solo Roth 401(k).

Plan C: John and Sandra Build Wealth with a Tax-Free Plan

In Plan A, John and Sandra did three quick real estate flip deals with after-tax money, paying tax as they went. In Plan B, we examined what would have happened if they had done the deals with tax-deferred IRA money through a Real Estate IRA LLC Plan. They still used a loan to finance most of the deal, had UDFI to consider, and took a tax hit when they pulled money from their tax-deferred plan. But the Solo Roth 401(k) plan isn't subject to UDFI tax on the leveraged portion. In Plan C, we'll figure out how a truly tax-free plan would work for flipping properties.

Let's review the income from John and Sandra's property sales

Home #1: The total gain was $25,000. There would be no tax due using the Real Estate Tax-Free Plan and a Solo Roth 401(k).

Home #2: The total gain was $35,500. Again, no tax due.

Home #3: The total gain was $30,000 with no tax due.

John and Sandra made a total of $90,500 from flipping the three homes. As with Plans A and B, they invested the money into something that had a 10 percent return and allowed it to compound and grow over a 20-year period. Let's contrast that with the money they made in regular investment Plan A and the tax-deferred Plan B.

	Comparing John and Sandra's Investment Options		
Investment Term	Plan A (After Tax)	Plan B (Tax-Deferred)	Plan C (Tax-Free)
5 Years	$ 62,000	$ 93,000	$146,000
10 Years	$ 84,000	$133,000	$235,000
15 Years	$116,000	$200,000	$378,000
20 Years	$159,000	$322,000	$609,000

Okay—now they're getting into retirement territory.

WHEN TAX-FREE DOESN'T MAKE SENSE

In all of our examples so far the tax-free investment comes out on top by a long margin. But if that was always the case, we wouldn't even be mentioning tax-deferred investing as an option. So it stands to reason, therefore, that there is a time and a place for tax-deferred investing.

But, when is that?

Well, first let's go back and review the different forms of taxes that you might encounter during your real estate investing activities. Then we'll see what happens when you add a Real Estate IRA strategy into the mix.

There are three basic types of federal taxes that you will pay in real estate transactions:

1. *Earned Income Tax.* If you buy and sell properties quickly (you hold them for one year or less), you're involved in a real

168

estate trade or business. In fact, under IRS rules you aren't even considered a real estate investor! Instead, the IRS views you as a real estate dealer who buys and sells properties. That means the money you make from this activity is considered earned income just as though you were a W-2 employee. Earned income is taxed at your ordinary tax rate, whatever that may be. If you aren't operating through a proper business structure but instead just flip properties in your own name you'll also have something called "self-employment tax," which is roughly equivalent to the payroll taxes that a proper business structure would pay.

2. *Long-Term Capital Gains Tax.* The long-term capital gains tax rate is the lowest federal tax rate. It applies to a property that you sell after owning it for one year or more. There is also a short-term capital gains tax that is applicable if you've held a property for less than one year. The short-term capital gains tax rate is the same as your ordinary income tax rate, but the money you earn in this instance isn't subject to self-employment tax. The difference between short-term capital gains and flipping properties is intent. If you intended to buy and sell the property within one year, the IRS will look at your profit as ordinary income. If you bought a property to hold for several years but had to sell for some unexpected reason, you can claim the profit as short-term capital gains instead. (The IRS has a whole series of reasons they will accept. We've set them out on our web site, www.reirallc.com).

3. *Passive Income Tax.* Passive income is the income that you make from the rents on your real estate. It is a different type of subcategory. You can apply passive losses against passive income, but generally passive losses are limited against earned income. Additionally, passive income can be offset by depreciation, which often completely wipes out any taxable income. Any passive income that remains after the depreciation and other deductions is taxed at the ordinary individual tax rate.

TAX-NOW, TAX-DEFERRED, OR TAX-FREE

If you use a tax-now strategy, you'll pay taxes on your real estate sales in the year the properties are sold. If you use a tax-deferred or tax-free IRA as part of your IRA LLC strategy, you can either defer or avoid the taxes from real estate.

Now, if you use a tax-deferred IRA, you won't pay tax on that income until you withdraw it from your pension—at rates of up to 35 percent. But if you had used a tax-now strategy instead (you bought the property directly, rather than through your pension) and the property was subject to a long-term capital gains rate, you could be paying as little as 15 percent when you sold it. So even though you pay tax now, you could be paying as much as 20 percent less than you would down the road.

Take Rachel C, for example. Rachel sold a property that gave her a gain of $100,000, which was subject to the long-term capital gains tax rate of 15 percent. (We're going to disregard the depreciation recapture calculation, which is taxed at a different rate, and the state income tax, just to keep the example very simple).

Plan A (Tax Now)	Plan B (Tax Later)
Rachel sells the property outside of a Real Estate IRA LLC. In other words, this is done either in her own name (not recommended) or through a regular LLC.	Rachel sells this inside a Real Estate IRA LLC. In this case, the underlying IRA is tax-deferred, so that she doesn't pay tax until the pension distributes.
Her gross profit is $100,000 less $15,000 (15 percent of $100,000). Rachel ends up with a net profit of $85,000	Her pension ends up with the $100,000 gross profit. If it immediately distributes the money, Rachel will have to pay the ordinary income tax rate, which in her case is at the maximum of 35 percent. This time, Rachel ends up with a net profit of only $65,000.

In this case, it makes more sense to use a tax-now plan. The 15 percent capital gains rate was better for Rachel than the 35 percent ordinary income tax rate.

But, is that always the case? What if you wait a few years and then take the money out?

Plan A (Five Years Out)	Plan B (Five Years Out)
Take the $85,000 and invest it at 10 percent, fully taxable. In five years, you'd have $116,457.	Take the $100,000 and, instead of distributing it, leave it in your pension and invest it at 10 percent, tax-deferred. In five years, you'd have $141,511. Of course, you still have to pay tax on that when you distribute the money.

Which is the best wealth-building plan—to go fully taxable or tax deferred? The answer is "it depends."

If you have time to wait, you'll be better off with the tax-deferred money. And if you have the money already in a plan, get it working for you better and faster with good real estate deals. Otherwise, if you're looking for quick cash to pay the bills, it might make more sense to just do it with all after-tax money and forgo the RE IRA plans.

Make tax planning part of your real estate investments. If you do, you'll find that you can make more money, faster, than you ever thought possible.

SECTION SIX

Business Tips, Real Estate Flips, and Power Trips

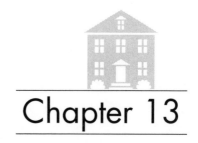

Chapter 13

WHAT KIND OF REAL ESTATE SHOULD YOU BUY (AND HOW DO YOU FIND IT)?

Generally there are two financial rewards from investing in real estate. One is the cash flow you get from rental income. We like the rental income to exceed expenses such as the mortgage payment, property taxes, insurance, and maintenance, in which case you end up with positive cash flow.

The second financial reward of investing in real estate stems from the fact that in general real estate goes up in value. This capital appreciation means that your equity, or what you own in the property, continually increases.

In general, where cash flow returns are high, capital growth tends to be somewhat lower. Similarly, where you have high capital growth, you tend to get lower cash flow returns. The question as to whether you should go with a property with high capital growth or high cash flow returns depends on your circumstances. For instance, a neurosurgeon earning $800,000 a year will probably not be too concerned with the cash flow from a property and has the luxury of looking for real estate that can generate spectacular capital growth. Conversely, a young beginner investor with no or little income may be forced to acquire real estate with lower capital growth, but with high cash flow returns for the simple reason that the beginner cannot sustain any period of negative cash flow.

Where you as an investor fall on this spectrum will depend on your income level, your marital status, the number of dependents, your age, your job security, and the extent to which you are risk-averse. (Can you sleep at night knowing you've got a large mortgage and not much positive cash flow even though the anticipation is that your property will double in value in the next few years?)

Whichever kind of property you want to buy or are interested in, you have to understand that real estate is a numbers game. What this means is that you have to look at a lot of properties to find one that meets your criteria. In Dolf's book, *Real Estate Riches*, he describes in some detail the 100-10-3 Rule. In essence, what this rule entails is that you have to expect to look at 100 pieces of real estate in order to find 10 that you might be interested in putting offers on. When you put offers in on 10 properties, you cannot expect all 10 offers to be accepted. (In fact, if all 10 offers *were* accepted, that would be an indication you are offering too much.) Of the 10 submitted offers, maybe only 3 are accepted. Even this does not mean that you can buy 3 properties, because you still have to fund them. Maybe you can only get funding for 1 of them. In this case, you would have looked at 100 properties in order to buy 1. This won't always be the case. However, a very common phenomenon we see is that new investors look at maybe three or four properties and then hastily come to the conclusion that everything they've read in a book or learned in a course is hyped-up nonsense because the formulas simply don't work. Don't fall into this trap. Accept that you have to look at a lot of properties to find a few great deals.

When considering acquiring real estate, most people think in terms of listings through a real estate company or looking in the newspaper. There is nothing wrong with these two methods. In fact, they probably precipitate the bulk of real estate transactions. However, they are by no means the only sources of investment real estate. One of the smartest things you can do is to go out and print new business cards with your name on them, and underneath your name, in a large font (bigger than your name), put the words REAL ESTATE INVESTOR.

This serves two purposes. First, every time you hand out a card, it lets the recipient know your focus is on investing in real estate. Second, and perhaps more important, it reminds you every time you hand out a card that this is in fact what you do.

As you are driving around town, keep an eye out for FSBO signs (For Sale By Owner) as these properties are not listed for sale by any real estate companies and usually are not in an electronic database. Furthermore, the fact that these people have opted to sell these properties themselves means that they may have done the appraisal themselves. Very often, their own estimate of value of their property is way above market, but often their estimate is way below market. In other words, FSBOs can be a great source of advantageously priced real estate.

We once had a taxi driver complain to us that since he was forced to work two shifts, he had no time left over to look for real estate. While we are not sure on the legalities of working two shifts, when we pointed out that he spent some 12 hours a day driving around town, and that he therefore had a good chance of being one of the first people to observe a new FSBO—sign, his demeanor improved remarkably.

Furthermore, if while searching for real estate, you liberally hand out your newly printed business cards, you will be surprised how often you'll get phone calls from people either with real estate for sale, or who know of a piece of real estate for sale. ("Hey, aren't you the guy who buys real estate? Well, I just went to stay at my cousin's house at the beach, and the house next door has a FOR SALE sign on it. I think the person who owned it passed away and it could be a good deal.")

One of the most important things to consider when looking for real estate is to have a strategy. If you are willing to look at anything so long as it is technically real estate, your mind will end up spinning at the endless and confusing options. Know exactly what it is you are after. If you are interested in residential real estate, what kind of residences? Free-standing single-family homes, or multi-unit apartments? Old or new? A maximum of two bedrooms, or a minimum of five? With or without a swimming pool? In which specific Zip Codes? If you know exactly what it is you are looking for, it will be much easier to find. Furthermore, by writing your strategy on a sheet of paper, you can give a copy to the various real estate agents and other people you come across, who can then lead you to deals you are interested in, and not waste your time with deals that fall outside your criteria.

Whatever the category of real estate you want to pursue, you have to decide if you want to expend any energy improving the property. The downside of making any improvements is that it can take a lot of time and energy—time and energy that could otherwise be spent finding the next great deal. However, many people cannot see that with a relatively small amount of effort, great value can be added to a property.

We firmly believe there are 101 things you can do to massively increase the value of your real estate without spending much money—so much so that one of us has written a book with that exact title: *101 Ways to Massively Increase the Value of Your Real Estate without Spending Much Money* (Time Life Direct). While we will not repeat its contents here, we will highlight some of the concepts to make you understand how it is possible to increase the value of real estate by much more than the cost of the improvement.

One of the most obvious ways you can improve a house is simply to paint it (in fact, if you're really cheap, you can probably get away with just painting the front of the house, although we do not think this is very wise). Geraniums or other colored flowers in window boxes may cost a grand total of $40, but can easily add a thousand dollars to the value of a property. It may not be rational that $40 worth of plants can increase the value of a property by $1,000, but if it does increase the value by that much, then surely it is wise to spend the $40.

Similarly, replacing a dilapidated mail box can increase the overall value by much more than the cost of the mail box. Another great idea is to replace low wattage light bulbs with much brighter light bulbs in the rooms. This can make the rooms seem bigger, brighter, fresher, and cleaner, all for the sake of 99 cents per bulb (or less if bought in bulk at Costco).

While these are simple and relatively cheap things to do, there are many ideas at the other end of the spectrum. Spending $25,000 remodeling a kitchen may increase the value of a house by $100,000. A new bathroom or an additional bedroom may do the same.

The trick is to know what to do to each particular house. This is where the old adage "buy the worst house on the best street" comes into play, because such a house will enable you to be very creative when it comes to improvements.

For people starting in real estate, we recommend the single-family home as a sound investment choice for the simple reason the majority of Americans live in single-family homes and therefore the pool of potential tenants is the largest. To be sure, most single-family homes have items that require a lot of maintenance, such as front yards, backyards, fences, and sometimes swimming pools. However, especially when tenants are indeed families, the properties are usually well maintained.

Another category is duplexes, triplexes, or even more units, under one roof. These have certain advantages over single-family homes. In particular, you have the benefit of multiple rental income streams. Furthermore, as you get more units under one roof, the returns tend to go up. However, in general, the management overhead in multifamily units rises exponentially. This is because in general, single-family homes tend to attract families, while multiple units tend to attract younger tenants with less job stability who are still going in and out of relationships, and who tend to be more itinerant. As a consequence, they throw more parties. You'll get more calls from the noise abatement department of your local city council. You'll get complaints from the lady in upstairs Unit Seven about the bozos downstairs in Unit Two who have too many cars in the parking lot.

Whatever the disadvantages and advantages of different kinds of residential real estate, there are investors for all categories. Your task is to determine which category you want to specialize in, and then focus on that category so that you can become very successful at it.

Single-family homes and multifamily units probably cover around 95 percent of residential accommodation. However, there are many other forms of real estate that are worthy of investment. Commercial real estate covers a wide range of categories, including office towers, shopping centers, strip malls, industrial buildings, factories, police stations, hospitals, car yards, funeral parlors, convenience stores, car washes, water treatment stations, and so on and so forth. Furthermore, there are odd categories of real estate that serious investors never overlook. Just as an example, we will talk about air space, which is a category most people never consider.

Air space is very valuable. Consider a two-story building that has been constructed with foundations strong enough to carry a ten-story building. The airspace may be sold to a buyer who wants to build another eight stories. There are however many other uses for airspace besides physically constructing something in that space.

Consider a 30-story apartment building overlooking the beach or a lake or a nice park. If there is a small building between the apartment tower and the beautiful view, then it would be very wise to acquire the airspace above the single-story building to prevent anything being built that would block the views from the apartment building.

Similarly, airspaces may be acquired to maintain a view not *from* a building, but *of* the building. One of us was recently involved in acquiring a commercial building in Sydney, Australia, where $523,000 of rental income came from a billboard on top of the 14-story building. This billboard could be seen for many miles from a major arterial road leading into downtown Sydney. In this case, it was beneficial to acquire the air rights over the building next door to prevent views of the billboard from being obstructed. (At a cap rate of 10 percent, the billboard was worth more than $5 million.)

Rooftop space may also be leased out to put in cellular phone towers, other communication towers, weather or traffic cams for local television stations, satellite dishes to service local offices, pollution monitoring stations, or helipads. Similarly, you could sell the naming rights to a building.

The whole point is that sometimes by spending little money, and often times by spending no money at all, you can dramatically increase the value of a piece of real estate. You are only limited by your imagination.

One of the biggest challenges when looking for potential real estate investments is to avoid falling in love with a property. It is tempting to think, *That house is so cute*, or *My friends will be so impressed if I can tell them that I own that big glass office tower.* These are not sound reasons to buy either property. At the end of the day, real estate is a numbers game. Do the numbers work for you? Fall in love with the deal, not the property.

To help you make wise decisions as to whether the numbers work, and to help you get through the 100 properties you need to look at on average to find 1 great deal (the 100-10-3-1 Rule), it is smart to automate the process. We have developed and refined software to analyze real estate (specifically to determine if we should acquire the property or not). Our Real Estate Acquisition Program (REAP) takes all the numeric variables associated with a piece of investment real estate as input data. These variables include the purchase price, market value, rental levels, vacancy rates, management fees, mortgage interest rate and terms, maintenance, and property taxes, to name just some. It then processes the data to show you how this investment will impact you, based on your income level, tax rate, and capital base. REAP also allows you to easily compare several potential investment properties, even if they have vastly different prices, rentals, and mortgages associated with them, to find our which one or ones you should acquire.*

If looking at potential real estate deals is drudgery to you, then it will be difficult to consistently find great investment opportunities. However, if you like the uncertainty of not knowing what you may find around the next corner, if you like analyzing deals and figuring out what you may do to a property to increase its value beyond the cost of making the improvement, and if you enjoy either working directly with real estate or managing someone who does it for you, then you have caught the fever. Choose which category of real estate you want to be involved with, work the market, let your creativity run rife, and have fun doing it.

---

*More information on REAP can be found at www.dolfderoos.com.

Chapter 14

WHAT KIND OF BUSINESSES SHOULD YOU BUY (AND HOW DO YOU DO IT)?

This book is titled *The Insider's Guide to Tax-Free Real Estate Investments,* which might make you wonder why we're talking about investing in businesses. There are really two reasons why:

1. Sometimes real estate investing becomes business investing when you invest in other companies that buy, renovate, manage, and/or sell real estate.
2. There is so much misinformation in the marketplace that limits knowledge about pension investing; this is our chance to correct some of that information.

First, let's say what should be the mantra for pension investing. Unless it's a prohibited transaction or prohibited investment, you can probably do it with your pension. But there are going to be more paperwork requirements. Fail to follow the rules, and you run the risk of that 50 percent additional excise tax.

WHAT BUSINESSES CAN YOU BUY?

All kinds! You can buy and operate an existing business with your pension plan. You can invest pension money into an existing business and sit as a passive background investor. It can be a private business or a huge public corporation. You can even start a business with your pension plan.

Now, let's look at some of the pros and cons of buying into a business with your pension fund.

PRIVATE PLACEMENTS

A private placement is the term used for pension investing in a nonpublic offering. That's basically what is happening most of the time when you use your pension money to invest in a business. Generally, the business is a private company with not many shareholders.

There are two issues to watch for when you invest in a business:

1. Entering into a prohibited transaction.
2. Incurring UBIT.

PROHIBITED TRANSACTION CONSIDERATIONS FOR BUSINESSES

When IRA funds are invested in a business interest in which the IRA owner has, or will have, some type of relationship, the prohibited transaction label may arise. Remember, if a prohibited transaction occurs within your pension plan, you must pay immediate tax on the entire value of your pension—not just the amount you invested in the problem transaction.

We talked about the relationships that can trigger prohibited transactions earlier. Those are transactions that occur when you (the pension owner) are also a current owner, co-investor, employee, creditor, director, or officer of the business your pension is investing in. It's also possible for a prohibited transaction to occur after the investment is made if a transaction occurs or services are performed by you.

If you're not sure if a transaction might be considered a prohibited transaction, open a separate self-directed IRA account to make the investment. That way the worst thing that can happen is you might end up having to pay tax on the amount that is invested in that particular venture. You won't put all of your main pension investments at risk for tax.

An important tax court case, *Rollins v. Commissioner,* addressed the case of a pension plan that wholly funded a money fund. Some of the loans went to organizations that benefited the pension plan owner and fiduciary.

This case is significant because it contradicted previous case law when it ruled that a prohibited transaction (due to disqualified persons) had occurred. The case seemed to hang on which was more significant:

- The fact that a loan made by a company which was owned by an IRA made a loan to another entity that was only partially owned (33 percent) by the IRA owner.
- The fact that there was an indirect benefit to the IRA owner (who also happened to be the pension plan fiduciary).

Normally, it would take owning 50 percent or more in the second entity to trigger the prohibited transaction issue. In this case, although the IRA owner only held 33 percent ownership in the second entity, the main point, according to the court, was that there was a benefit to the IRA owner due to the loans.

As you can see, this area of the IRS regulations is not at all settled. That means current knowledge is essential if your LLC's transactions involve anyone but third parties in relation to your pension fund.

ROTH IRA INVESTMENTS IN BUSINESS

Sometimes you'll need to report certain business investments that your Roth IRA or your Tax-Free LLC (funded by your Solo Roth 401(k) plan) makes. Typically, these are transactions made between a business that is largely owned by a Roth IRA or Tax-Free LLC and another business that is also owned or run by the Roth IRA or Tax-Free LLC owners. These types of transactions are called "listed" transactions. They aren't illegal or prohibited, but you do need to give the IRS notice when you enter into one.

Due to past abuses by some major tax accounting firms, the IRS has clamped down on listed transactions through new regulations issued in IRS Notice 2004-8.* Make sure your plan's custodian and your financial advisors review these requirements before you make investments with your Roth plan. Again, remember—it doesn't mean you can't make the investment—it's just very important that there be no fraud or appearance of fraud in the eyes of the IRS.

---

*Do you want to know more? You can find a copy of this important notice, IRS Notice 2004-8, at our web site, www.reirallc.com.

UBIT AND BUSINESS INVESTMENTS

UBIT is similar to the UDFI tax that results when leverage is used for an investment in which the pension invests. We talked about UBIT and UDFI back in Chapter 12.

There are two possible business entities that might have a UBIT problem: the partnership and the limited liability company. These are the two flow-through entities that your pension can invest in. A flow-through entity is an entity that does not pay tax at its own level. Instead the taxable income flows through to the individual owners, called partners in a partnership and members in an LLC. Most pensions can't invest in an S Corporation, but the new Solo 401(k) and the Solo Roth 401(k) plans can. That's one more reason these new strategies are so compelling!

Diane's Story

I wish I could say this story happened to me. But, this is actually a story of a client of my self-directed IRA custodian.

One of his clients was involved in the beginning with a start-up that hoped to go public. He started with a small investment through his Roth account that was actually less than $2,000.

And, this investment turned into one of those golden dot.com booms. The stock went public and then another company bought them out. The price jumped. They were bought again, and the price jumped again. One more time, they were bought, and the stock price sky-rocketed.

That's when the client decided enough was enough. His less than $2,000 investment was now worth $6,000,000. How much tax does he owe on that huge gain? Nothing! He did it all through his Roth IRA.

If the business your pension has invested in produces or sells goods, or provides services, the income it makes will probably be subject to UBIT. Your pension's pro-rata share of that income will be subject to tax at the trust income tax rate. If the business obtained a loan to start or keep operating, your pension may also have to pay UBIT over the portion of the business's income that was earned because it incurred the debt.

If your pension invests in a C Corporation, there will be no UBIT issue. That's because C Corporations pay tax directly, at their own corporate tax rate, regardless of who or what owns shares in the C Corporation. And any dividends the C Corporation pays out to your pension will not be subject to UBIT. Additionally, if your pension fund sells the shares later, there will be no capital gains tax.

PROHIBITED TRANSACTIONS

There were potential issues when your pension plan invested in real estate. You had to be concerned about prohibited transactions, disqualified persons, and prohibited investments. The same issues occur when your pension plan invests in business. Let's look at some common business scenarios to determine if they would qualify as prohibited transactions if your business was involved.

- Your pension owns 100 percent of a company. The company pays you or your spouse a salary. The transaction is prohibited. Why? You and a similarly disqualified person are personally benefiting from the pension investment.
- Your pension owns 60 percent of a hedge fund. Your two sisters own the other 40 percent. You can take 40 percent of the usual market-rate management fee for operating the hedge fund. This represents the portion of the hedge fund

188

that you don't own. The transaction is not prohibited. Why? Your sisters wouldn't be considered disqualified persons because they aren't "line" relatives (parents, grandparents, children, grandchildren). However—and this is a big caveat—if your sisters are beneficiaries of the pension, they will be disqualified persons. In that case, the transaction would be prohibited.

- Your pension owns 100 percent of a motel. You receive a salary to operate the motel. The transaction is prohibited. Why? You are benefiting from an investment of the pension.
- Your pension owns 100 percent of a motel. You sell the motel, and all gain flows into your pension. This transaction is not prohibited. Why? Not only is it not prohibited, this is the type of sweet deal that you want to have happen!

STARTING A COMPANY

Your pension can invest, either alone or with other individuals or their pension funds in the private stock of a new start-up company. We strongly recommend that you use a qualified attorney to develop and implement this type of plan. The documents must be properly drawn to protect the integrity of the pension investment.

FINAL THOUGHTS ON INVESTING IN A BUSINESS WITH YOUR PENSION

This book was designed primarily for real estate investors looking for ways to create tax-advantaged income from their current real estate investments and for people wanting to build massive wealth quickly with real estate in their retirement funds. The strategies of investing in business are, frankly, a bit of an afterthought. But on the other hand, the possibilities are almost limitless for investing in business:

Private Stock in Closely Held Businesses.

Initial Public Offerings (IPOs).

Publicly Traded Stock.

Loans to Existing Businesses.

Purchases of New Business.

Start-up Businesses.

As long as you avoid prohibited transactions with your IRA, chances are the worst thing that can happen is that a portion of your pension will become subject to UBIT. At any rate, if you have a retirement plan already and are interested in seeing it grow more rapidly, ask yourself, with every investment: "Is this something I should be doing with my pension plan?"

Chapter 15

INVESTING BEYOND OUR BORDERS

The citizens of many foreign countries are acutely aware of fluctuating exchange rates, the vagaries of trade imbalances, and the effects of tariffs and trade incentives. This is because their daily cost of living is directly affected by these factors. For instance, since most countries do not manufacture cars, if their currency goes down by 5 percent, then cars (and a host of other imports) will rise in price by at least that much. Here in the United States, many people are blissfully insulated from and therefore unaware of these changing market conditions. In relative terms, we are so large and self-sufficient that not much changes if the value of the British pound or the Brazilian real goes up or down a little.

Therefore it will probably come as a surprise to most Americans that the value of the U.S. dollar, when measured against a trade-weighted basket of currencies, has gone down by more than 50 percent in the five years since October 2000. In other words, if an American investor had shipped a $1 million overseas in 2000, and repatriated it five years later, it would have been worth more than $2 million, even if it wasn't invested. If you believe it is possible the U.S. dollar may go down further, then investing beyond our borders may make a lot of sense. There are many other reasons that make investing abroad a good option for some people.

To be sure, there are many disadvantages of investing abroad—there are other rules and regulations to consider, different credit reporting systems to deal with, different terminology, and in some cases a different language.

For instance, many Americans investing across our southern border have had to deal with extreme difficulty in even obtaining a mortgage to buy real estate, a language barrier, and a rare but real history of annexation of foreign-owned real estate by the government. On the other hand, increasing proportions of Americans are experiencing the tremendous benefits of buying well-priced real estate in fun destinations that do not require an eight hour (or more) plane ride.

If your sole aim in investing abroad is to generate returns higher than you'd hope to get in the United States, then we would suggest that it's a long shot at best and the extra hassles may not justify the effort required. However, consider this. Many Americans work extremely hard for years at a time to afford a vacation abroad, which has to be paid for out of tax-paid money. If you truly love investing in real estate, why not indulge your passion abroad, reap the benefits of an exotic location, favorable exchange rates, and having your vacations paid for out of pre-tax dollars? (Of course technically it wouldn't be a vacation, but as they say, if you find a job that you love doing, you will never have to work another day in your life.) As an investor, not only can the world become your oyster, but you can own a part of it, too.

One compelling reason to invest abroad is to spread your investment risk. The relative fortunes of various countries ebb and flow with time, and from a global perspective, having all one's assets tied up in one economy may not always be very smart. A currency meltdown (think of Thailand and Argentina in the late 1990s), an oil crisis (1973), or a terrorism attack can severely impact a nation, and having your investment eggs spread around gives you options.

For most Americans contemplating investing abroad, we thoroughly recommend operating in a country where English is the *lingua franca*, especially for those investors who have no foreign language skills. However, just because a country speaks English doesn't mean you'll be well-understood. The United States has evolved a unique set of terms for real estate matters that are frequently different form the rest of the world. While Americans walk on a sidewalk, in most other English-speaking countries, people walk on a footpath. Whereas we lift the hood of a car to get to the engine, other people lift the bonnet. We pump gas, they pump petrol. Here is our cheat sheet for real estate terms.

U.S. Real Estate Terms	Non-U.S. Real Estate Terms
apartment	flat
appraisal	valuation
appraiser	valuer
attorney	solicitor
closing	settlement
condominium	apartment
county	shire or district
down payment	deposit
eminent domain	government requisition
foreclosure sale	mortgagee sale (sometimes known as mortgage-in-possession sale)
mail box	letter box

(Continued)

U.S. Real Estate Terms	Non-U.S. Real Estate Terms
property taxes	rates (not to be confused with interest rates; the City Council is the rating authority)
real estate	property
return on investment	yield
roommate	flatmate
seller carry-back	vendor finance
state (geographic region)	province
title company (to effect a closing)	conveyancing solicitor (to effect a settlement)
Zip Code	Postal Code

Note that these loose translations vary slightly from country to country. The point is not that there are differences, but rather that the differences are almost trivial, and that you should not use their existence as an excuse not to invest abroad.

Most Americans are intimately familiar with their FICO score. Your FICO score is in fact a combination of scores reported by three credit agencies (Experian, TRW, and Transunion). Everyone knows that a FICO score over 800 is excellent and that a low FICO score will hamper your ability to get credit. The concept and the implementation of the FICO score system is uniquely American. Other countries do not have such a system. This is based partially on the notion that when it comes to real estate lending it is not so much the person who forms collateral for the loan, but the piece of real estate being acquired. Consequently in general, with respect to financing a deal, it is easier for an American to invest abroad than it is for a foreign national to invest in the United States.

When it comes to borrowing money, we often get asked if it is wise to borrow money in the United States to invest abroad. Firstly, we don't believe there is a single U.S.-based bank that will use a piece of real estate located beyond the borders of the United States as security for a loan, for the simple and logical reason that in the event of nonpayment of the mortgage, it would be difficult to enforce remedial action. Many then ask if they should borrow against existing assets in the United States and deploy the funds thus released abroad. The answer is an emphatic "no." The risk of borrowing money in the United States and investing it overseas is that the exchange rate will go against you. For this reason, we always recommend borrowing money where the real estate is.

There is another interesting aspect to investing abroad that we wish to highlight. If you consider any profession other than real estate investing and you try to practice that profession abroad, you generally have to study, pass exams, and become certified in that country. This applies whether you are an airline pilot, physician, dentist, nurse, architect, electrician, X-ray technician, enforcement officer, attorney, dermatologist, loan officer, or even a real estate agent (and countless other professions). Consequently, with any of these professions, you cannot just go to another country and practice your trade.

However, as a real estate investor, not only can you go to other countries and practice your trade without needing a certificate, qualification, retraining or retooling, but foreign governments welcome you with open arms under the illusion that since you're an investor, you must be bringing money into the country. We say this is an illusion because as we pointed out a little while ago, it is not always smart to bring capital to a foreign country.

One of the advantages of investing abroad is that other countries often have benefits that do not even exist in the United States. For instance, in New Zealand, there is no capital gains tax. It is not on the statutes. Similarly there is no inheritance tax, death duties, or estate tax, there is unlimited deductibility of losses in one enterprise against profits in a related enterprise,

there is no income limit beyond which you cannot claim mortgage deductions, and it has some of the highest depreciation
rates in the world. These facts do not mean that all Americans
should invest in New Zealand, nor do they mean that no New
Zealander can benefit from investing in the United States. However, we've taken groups of investors to various countries including New Zealand, resulting not only in lucrative investments, but
in fun times as well.*

---

*For information on any up-coming tours, please go to our web site www
.dolfderoos.com.

SECTION SEVEN

It's Never Too Late

Chapter 16

WHAT IF YOU'RE 40+ AND HAVE NO PENSION?

et's compare two people: Allison who starts investing at age 20 and Beth who starts investing at age 40. They each put away $100 a month. Assuming they manage to get an 8 percent return on their invested capital, and assuming the investments grow tax-free, by the time they both reach the age of 65, it is seen that Beth has only accumulated $95,102, whereas Allison has accumulated the relatively massive $527,454. To be sure, Allison has put in an extra $24,000 ($100 a month for an extra 20 years). However, she has generated an extra $432,352 in her retirement fund. Obviously, the sooner you start investing for your retirement, the better off you will be.

To look at it another way, let's assume Charlie and Dan both retire at the age of 65 and that they each retire with $1 million. Charlie started investing at age 20 and Dan at age 40. To achieve their $1 million retirement fund, Charlie had to invest $189.59 a month, whereas Dan had to invest a whopping $1,051.50 a month. The benefits of starting early should be self-evident.

Generally people don't think about planning for their retirement until they are well into their forties. One of the of the challenges of waiting until you're in your forties is that you don't have that much time left to build up a substantial nest egg. Ideally, you want to start investing in your early twenties. The problem with that is that most people in their early twenties think they are infallible, immortal, and that they have all the time in the world to do whatever they want. As a consequence, very few people enter their forties with a sound investment portfolio behind them.

While there are obvious advantages of starting early, are you doomed to a retirement of poverty if you don't have a pension plan by the time you're in your forties? The answer is an emphatic "no." However, you do have to take action. Ignoring the problem will not solve it.

So if you are over 40 and you do not have a pension, what steps can you take?

First, you have to be very focused on developing your pension plan in a very short time. This means, more so than for a younger starter, that you cannot decide on a whim to go on an extensive vacation in Europe rather than putting your self-imposed minimum in a pension plan. Second, it will pay to focus on plans and endeavors that are likely to create cash fast rather than an endeavor that may have great long-term benefits more suited to younger investors. For instance, buying 200 acres of land in the hope that growth in that area over the next 40 years will drive prices up astronomically is a strategy better suited to a younger investor. Rather, the later starters might benefit by focusing on acquiring real estate that has a twist to it, in the sense that if you change something about the property, it can dramatically increase the value. These changes may include a zoning change (for example from residential to commercial), a change of use (for example from storage facilities to showroom space), a change of tenant (from a butcher shop to an upscale espresso bar with wifi Internet and foreign newspapers), a change of rent (for instance, if the seller hadn't reviewed the rent in more than 12 years and just by bringing the rent up to market level, the value of the building trebles), or any of hundreds of different improvements you could make to a property along the lines of what was discussed in Chapter 13. Of course, there is nothing to stop the 20-year-old investor from acquiring properties like this, either. However, generally speaking, people only go to some effort if they have some specific incentive to do so. Investors in their forties have the real incentive of limited time.

Of course, those in their forties do have some advantages over the younger set. Apart from the wisdom and caution borne from having been burnt a few times, generally speaking, those in their forties have some material assets which may well turn out to be beneficial for their real estate investing. For example, if a forty-something year-old investor lives in an owner-occupied home with equity in it, this equity can be used as the down payment on an investment property. Similarly a jet ski, snowmobile, complete darkroom setup, RV, yacht, and sports car may be sold (you weren't really using these things anyway) to generate sufficient cash for the down payment on yet another deal.

Furthermore, most mature people tend to have a credit history which serves them and aids them in their investing endeavors greater than that enjoyed by a young 20-year-old with hardly any credit history.

We have both heard of people up in years who say they are too young to get started and relatively young people who say they are too old to get started. Whatever your age, there is no time like the present, and through the magic effects of compounding, starting today will make your life much easier than starting tomorrow. So it is incumbent on all of us, no matter what our age, to get serious about looking after our retirement. A Forbes report that just came out this week as we write, claims that 75 percent of people who have reached the age of 50 have got less than $5,000 saved towards their retirement.

When you consider that the proportion of elderly people is increasing, and that therefore there are fewer and fewer people working and paying income tax to support the increasing numbers of retired people who expect to get Social Security payments, it becomes all the more compelling to get started straight away.

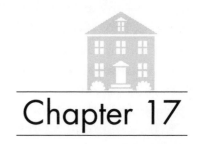

Chapter 17

WHAT IF YOU'VE GOT ALL YOUR MONEY TIED UP IN A TRADITIONAL 401(k)?

A lot of Americans have just two assets:

1. The equity in their home.
2. Their 401(k) plan from work.*

While many of these people would love to invest in real estate, they simply lack the funds to get started. And, even though we

---

*Throughout this chapter, we'll refer to the employer pension plan as a "401(k)." Your employer may have a different plan such as a 403(b); however, the same general principles will also apply to these other types of employer plans.

both know it is quite possible to buy real estate with little or even no money down, it is necessary to put a lot of time into those kinds of deals. If you're already struggling with a busy work and family life, the little or no money down deals just don't work for you. So what can you do?

If this sounds familiar to you, or someone you know, then this chapter is one you'll want to pay close attention to.

COUNT YOUR ASSETS

Do you have money hidden away in your attic or maybe in accounts that you barely remember? We all dream of finding hidden treasure. In some ways, that is exactly what you're doing now. You're on a treasure hunt. You're looking for the cash that can get you going in real estate investments.

List all of the things you own and how much equity (that's the difference between the asset's value and any debt you owe on

Connie did an assessment of the assets she owned. The first thing she noticed was the amount of equity that had built up in her home. She'd owned the home for over 10 years and, as time went by, her mortgage had been reduced by all those monthly payments. Plus, her house had gone up in value. That difference was equity.

Connie now had a couple of options she could use to access the cash that had built up in her house. She could get a second loan to tap into the home equity—these are often called HELOCs (home equity line of credit)—or she could refinance her first mortgage to pull the equity out. Connie also had a 401(k) plan that she intended to just keep in place until she made better use of the underutilized asset built up in her house.

that asset) you have in each of those items. It could be that you don't even have to worry about accessing your pension fund at first. There might be other cash to invest with that you want to use first.

TAPPING INTO YOUR 401(k)

Let's say that you have cash built up in your 401(k) plan that you'd like to use for real estate investing. How do you do that?

One idea is to get a loan against the balance in your account. If you're still working for the employer that has the 401(k), this may indeed be your only option because you can't roll the 401(k) into a self-directed plan, and the rules for a 401(k) preclude you from self-directing. Before you contact your plan administrator to get the paperwork going, make sure you thoroughly weigh the consequences of getting such a loan.

The problem with taking a loan is that if you leave employment for any reason, you must repay the loan. If you don't, it will be considered an early distribution and that means you'll pay tax plus a 10 percent early distribution penalty.

DISTRIBUTIONS FROM A 401(K)

You know already that there is a 10 percent penalty tax for early distributions from your pension plan. But there are some exceptions to this penalty. You can take penalty-free distributions for the following reasons:

- Your severance from employment, death or disability.
- Your employer terminates the plan.
- You reach age $59\frac{1}{2}$ (for some plans).

- You experience a substantial financial hardship (such as un-planned medical expenses).

Most 401(k) distributions occur when an employee leaves his or her job.

CHANGING JOBS

If you have money vested in a 401(k) plan and you change jobs, you must decide whether to:

- Leave the money in your former employer's 401(k) plan.
- Transfer the money into your new employer's plan (if one exists).
- Transfer the money to a self-directed IRA (or other type of pension) account.

If your goal is to invest in real estate, then you'll need a self-directed plan. And that means you'll need to follow the final option above: transfer the money to an IRA account or, better yet, start a business and transfer that money into your own Solo 401(k) plan.

ROLLING INTO A SELF-DIRECTED PLAN

Once you've decided to rollover into a self-directed plan, there are still more options you'll need to choose from.

Rolling into a traditional IRA. There will be no tax consequences as long as you follow the rules for rollovers. If you take out a cash distribution, remember you only have 60 days to get it redeposited into your new IRA account. Get a good custodian who can help you make the transfer, set up an LLC to hold the investment and you're rolling!

Roll into a Roth IRA. If you convert into a Roth IRA, you'll have some immediate tax consequences as you'll pay tax on the immediate value of the pension plan. There are also some income limitations on this strategy.*

Roll into a Solo 401(k). There is an additional first step for the Solo 401(k) conversion strategy. You must have a small business that will qualify to set up a Solo 401(k). The advantage of a Solo 401(k) over a regular 401(k) is that you can self-direct. And the advantage of the Solo 401(k) rollover strategy versus a traditional IRA rollover is that the Solo 401(k) investments will not be subject to UDFI for leveraged properties.

It's more trouble to have a Solo 401(k), and if you don't want to have a small business, it might actually not be possible for you. But if you can do it, the Solo 401(k) eliminates the major issue of IRA investing in real estate.

Roll into a Solo Roth 401(k). To add in one more decision to the rollover process, you could also roll your 401(k) into a Solo Roth 401(k). You'll still need a business that can qualify for a Solo 401(k) plan, and in this case, you'll also need to meet the income qualification for a conversion to a Roth.

If you can qualify, you'll also need to set up a Tax Free LLC. Then you can get ready to make money and *never* pay tax!

---

*For the latest tax planning techniques for Roth IRA conversions, please go to www.reirallc.com.

THE NEXT STEP

Accessing the funds is one thing, now you have to find and successfully manage the investments. There is no substitute for solid skills in real estate investing. Make sure you take the time to get the education first before you put your pension money at risk.

Chapter 18

IS REAL ESTATE OVER?

THE BUBBLE THAT NEVER WAS

As we write this, mortgage interest rates are on the rise, house sales are slowing, foreclosures are on the increase, and there is a general sentiment that the real estate market could be about to collapse.

This general doom and gloom has been exacerbated, if not brought on, by the media intent on selling news coverage with sensational headlines and stories. The headline, "Is the Bubble about to Burst?" may sell copy and advertising space, but it is arrogant, because it assumes that there is a bubble in the first place.

The media is quick to claim that there is a bubble in real estate. Forget for a moment that the stock market may decline 20 percent or 30 percent in a week, and the pundits and commentators merely say things like "there has been a minor correction in the stock market as profits are taken, but we expect that with next week's announcement of job statistics, the slack will be taken up," or something equally inane. When the real estate market comes down by even 5 percent, the reporters dive in like vultures proclaiming imminent and sustained real estate doom.

One of the main reasons why the bubble does not exist is that we have population inflation. We are not referring to the individuals getting larger, although that is a real phenomenon that is also part of a national trend. There is an excess of births and immigration over deaths and emigration. Currently, the population of the United States is estimated to be around 296 million. It is expected to exceed 350 million within 40 years. The population of California is expected to double in the next 25 years. One hundred houses are being built (and occupied) every day in Phoenix. The same goes for Las Vegas, despite the slight slow down there. Every week, a whopping 15,000 green cards are issued to new residents. It is estimated that every night, 1,500 illegal immigrants cross the border into Arizona. They say that one million illegal immigrants come into Texas every year. And here is the interesting thing. If you look around Phoenix at night, or anywhere in Arizona, or Texas, or anywhere else, you do not see hundreds of new arrivals, legal or illegal, sleeping on park benches and under overpasses. They are, with a few exceptions, all accommodated somewhere—in apartments, in houses, in some form of residential accommodation. This creates what is known as demand inflation: it puts upward pressure on prices. And as long as the population continues to increase, through the natural forces of supply and demand, prices will continue to increase.

By way of contrast to the increasing population of the United States, the population of Japan is in decline. Presently estimated at 124 million, it is expected that within a generation, the population will fall to under 100 million. This of itself will put downward pressure on real estate prices.

It is our opinion that the media are so keen to "prove" the imminent Bursting of the Bubble, that they use statistics in, at best, a very naive way.

"STATISTICS ARE JUST A GROUP OF NUMBERS LOOKING FOR AN ARGUMENT"

An *Economist* article dated June 16, 2005, studied real estate markets in the United States, Great Britain, and Australia. The authors concluded the markets were close to crashing. What is interesting is the way they graphed their data. They showed the annual appreciation rate. Appreciation slowed, but remained positive with *no fall* in capital value. To the casual observer, however, things did not look good.

Figure 18.1 is the chart that the *Economist* ran in June 2005, to prove their point that a house price (appreciation) decline heralded the arrival of their promised bubble (the same one they promised in 2004).

It is seen that the average annual British appreciation rate dropped from a high of 26 percent in mid 2002 to a manageable 6 percent in mid 2005. In the same period, the Australian annual

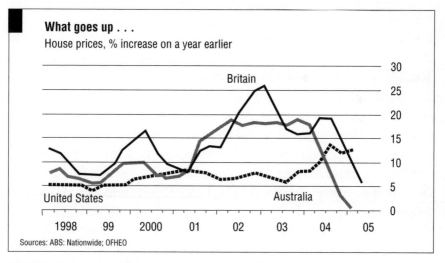

What goes up . . .
House prices, % increase on a year earlier

Britain

United States　　　　　　　　　　Australia

1998　　99　　2000　　01　　02　　03　　04　　05

Sources: ABS: Nationwide; OFHEO

FIGURE 18.1　Annual House Price Appreciation Trends
Source: The Economist, June 16, 2005.

average dropped from a sizzling 19 percent to .05 percent, but still remained positive. Over the same three years the annual U.S. trend has risen from about 6 percent to 12 percent.

First, this is far from the disaster the chart could be interpreted to show. House prices *did not drop* at any time in any of the three countries! At worst, the appreciation rate merely slowed. In the first two cases it slowed while the United States is still showing appreciation.

- The British have seen three years of compounding appreciation, 26 percent + 16 percent + 6 percent or a total of 55 percent or a manageable 18.3 percent a year.
- Australia has seen three years of compounding appreciation, 19 percent + 18 percent + .05 percent or a total of 47 percent for an even more manageable 15.8 percent a year.
- America has averaged a consecutive 7 percent, 6 percent and 12 percent or 27.0 percent for an annual average of 9.0 percent over the same period.

THE SAME DATA, REDRAWN TO REFLECT THE REAL GAIN

Let's see if there is a different way to display the data that looks so fatalistic in the *Economist*. We recreated their data in our own spreadsheet and graph as in Figure 18.2.

It shows essentially the same data: We entered the data read from their graph.

However, instead of showing annual increases, it makes far more sense for us to graph cumulative increases, as house prices do in fact increase cumulatively.

Notice how Figure 18.3, based on exactly the same data set, gives a much rosier impression: what is seen now is that the rate

House price increases

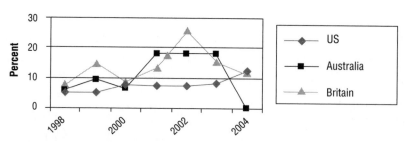

FIGURE 18.2   Our Version of the Same Raw Data

Cumulative house price increases

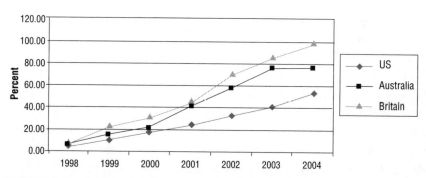

FIGURE 18.3   The Same Data Expressed as Cumulative Numbers

of growth has slowed a little, or, in the case of Australia, has leveled off for the last year.

However, appealing as the graph in Figure 18.3 is, it is still not an accurate picture, as it takes no account of the compounding nature of the data. If a $100,000 house increases by 10 percent for each of two years, the end value is not $120,000, but rather $121,000 because of compounding. The next graph shows the actual growth, taking compounding effects into consideration (see Figure 18.4).

Compounding house price increases

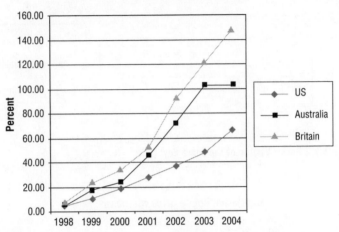

FIGURE 18.4 The Same Data Taking Compounding Effects into Consideration

Impressive as Figure 18.4 is, even this one does not show the typical picture for most homeowners and investors, as nearly all real estate investments are leveraged, meaning that they have a mortgage for a portion of the purchase price. If you consider that the average property is about 50 percent mortgaged in this country, then our next graph shows the effect of leverage (Figure 18.5).

Just so that you can see the dramatic difference between the original *Economist* graph and our own, we have recreated the statistics for the United States on one chart, comparing this time— for the United States only—the simple growth rates, the cumulative growth rates, the compounding growth rates, and the growth in equity. (See Figure 18.6.)

This is what we mean when we say statistics are just a group of numbers looking for an argument. Most people shown the *Economist* graph would be tempted to conclude that the bubble was indeed about to burst. Most people shown our final graph—the build up of equity—would be inspired to get into real estate then and there. You must always temper statistics with solid and sound

**Compounding Equity Increases
assuming 50% leverage**

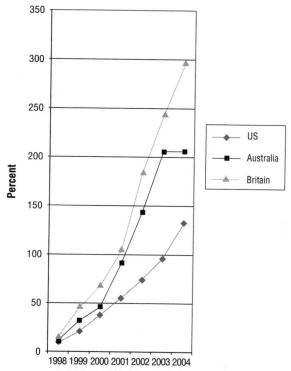

FIGURE 18.5 Compounding Effects with 50 Percent Mortgage

reasoning. We have written more extensively on Bubble Bursting in a Special Report *Bubble-proof Your Real Estate Investments* (published by *Personal Real Estate Investor Magazine*, 2005).*

A crash of some sort is still possible. However, the event that triggers any economic contraction will not be overpriced

---

*Copies of *Bubble-Proof Your Real Estate Investments* are available at www.dolfderoos.com and www.personalrealestateinvestormag.com.

Results for the US

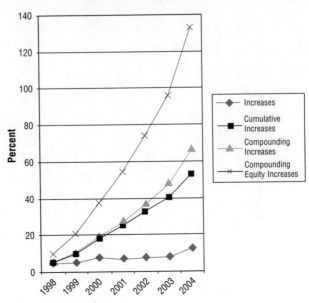

FIGURE 18.6 Composite U.S. Results

housing, but rather a collection of external pressures such as contracting or expensive energy supplies exacerbated by extremely destructive weather like Hurricane Katrina or another terrorist attack.

SHOULD YOU CONTINUE TO INVEST IN REAL ESTATE?

Despite all the public talk about the impending bursting of the real estate bubble and the general feeling of doom and gloom that surrounds that talk, we believe there are compelling reasons why it is justified to have faith that real estate will continue to do well.

Compared with the Stock Market, Real Estate Is Very Safe

Companies can rise in value very quickly. Some notable examples are Google and eBay, which not too many years ago did not even exist, and today are worth billions of dollars. By the same token, companies can fall in value very quickly too, and often go under (bankrupt!). When they collapse, all the stockholders' funds disappear with them. We only have to look at the stock market listings from 20 years ago, or even 10 years ago, to realize that companies do not always last long. Some are merged into others (such as Compaq computers into HP), but many literally disappear. Does anyone remember the name Montgomery Ward? And what about Tyco, WorldCom, or Enron? Billions of stockholders funds have gone with them.

Of course, it is possible to lose real estate too. There are several mechanisms: fires, earthquakes, tornadoes, floods, and eminent domain, a process whereby the government deems it necessary to take possession of your real estate for some government-related purpose such as a new freeway. However, if the government wants to use eminent domain to requisition your property, they cannot just confiscate it from you without compensation! They must pay you fair market value. Further, you can get insurance to cover yourself against the risk of fire, earthquakes, tornadoes, floods, and other natural disasters. How many Enron stockholders had (or could get) insurance to cover themselves against the company being wiped out?

What is more, a significant number and proportion of companies do go under, whereas only a tiny fraction of real estate is lost through natural disasters or eminent domain, and even then there is usually compensation or insurance cover.

HISTORY CAN BE A GOOD INDICATION OF WHAT WILL HAPPEN IN THE FUTURE

Liz Ann Sonders, chief investment strategist for Charles Schwab & Co and a White House consultant, reports that "the national median home price has never fallen in a calendar year since the Great Depression." This is a very significant fact. Despite a World War, the Korean War, the Vietnam War, the two Gulf Wars, the Bay of Pigs fiasco, the oil crisis of 1973, the assassination, resignation, and impeachment of Presidents, the stock market crash of 1987, the Tech Wreck of 2000, and countless other significant world events, all of which have sent stock markets, commodities markets, and currency markets into tailspins, the national median home price has continued to march steadily upward. To anyone but the most ardent detractors of real estate, this gives a good level of confidence that despite future world events and ongoing gyrations in other markets, the real estate market is likely to continue its steady rise upward.

Of course many detractors of real estate point out that homes are relatively illiquid assets and can't be traded or liquidated in as instantaneous a fashion as stocks. Perhaps that is its very advantage: real estate is not very liquid, therefore people do not trade it as whimsically as other assets (and get burnt out at their computer monitors watching the value of their real estate fluctuate on a day-by-day or hour-by hour basis, with their fingers poised over the "sell" button).

It Is easy to Beat the Average in Real Estate

We are always amused at the number of mutual fund managers who boast, "For the last two years, we beat the X index by 15 percent. What happened in the two years prior to that? Stock market indexes fluctuate wildly and dramatically, and the values of individual stocks fluctuate even more wildly and dramatically. Beating the average consistently—the Holy Grail of many investment advisors—is difficult to do. In fact, we have not come across any credible strategy or formula to beat the average in the stock market.

On the other hand, we believe it is easy to beat the average in real estate confidently and consistently, and that our strategy stands up to scrutiny. Furthermore, you do not need to engage expensive advisors to learn, understand or apply the strategy.

Last year, the average capital growth of real estate was 9.7 percent. There are two things to note. First, this national average capital growth rate tends to change slowly over time (mathematically, the standard deviation is very low). Second, the capital growth rate of regional markets tends to also change very slowly, and in general unison with the national market (this contrasts dramatically with the stock market, where individual stocks can gyrate wildly and with no necessary correlation to the already volatile average).

How can we use these two features to beat the average consistently and with confidence?

Some regions have a lower than average capital growth rate. For instance, a county in Pennsylvania where a steel mill (which employed 56 percent of the county's workers) has closed down, is likely to suffer from a below-average real estate market (as workers move elsewhere in search of work). For the national average to be what it is, there has to be another part of the country where growth is above average. And since real estate trends are very slow, the regions that grow at below average or above average rates are likely to do so for long periods at a time.

Take Las Vegas, for instance. For eight years running, Las Vegas has been by most measures the number one city for growth in the United States. The growth rate of Las Vegas reached an all-time high in 2003, when the average annual compounding growth rate was a seemingly impossible 53.7 percent. Since then it has slowed dramatically to a much more sedate 27 percent per annum. Detractors of real estate were quick to point out that the more than 50 percent growth was unsustainable, but the whole point is that growth in Las Vegas, even when it came off the top by nearly 50 percent (to 27 percent), was still around three times the national average.

Now we know that the greatest test of will power is to refrain from saying, "I told you so," but one of us had been predicting that Vegas had to "pop" for the six years leading up to that massive increase. And, being ones to put our money where our mouths are, we set out to buy one house a week for an entire year in Las Vegas (documented in the book *52 Homes in 52 Weeks*, John Wiley & Sons, 2006).

Since the average growth rate in Las Vegas has been so much higher than the national average for many years, it is reasonably safe to assume that it will remain higher for a few more years to come. In other words, one way of beating the average is to invest in Las Vegas. However, within Las Vegas (just as within any city), there are suburbs that grow at higher than the city average growth rate, and suburbs that grow at lower than the city average growth rate (remember, that's how averages come about!). Similarly, within high-growth suburbs, there are clusters of streets that grow at higher than the suburb average, and clusters of streets that grow at lower than the suburb average (these streets may border a park, or follow a ridge affording the houses on those streets magnificent views out to sea).

Geographically, you can beat the average not just by choosing the right city to invest in, but by choosing the right suburb and even clusters of streets within a suburb. By way of example, in Las Vegas, where the average growth rate was 53.7 percent the year we were investing heavily there, many of our investments were in a suburb called Summerlin (named after the maiden name of the mother of Howard Hughes, who had been buying vast tracts of land there). The annual capital growth of our homes in Summerlin that year was over 80 percent.

Clearly, you can beat the average in real estate by choosing the correct geography. However, there are many other strategies that can result in similar above-average results. Dolf's book *Real Estate Riches* (John Wiley & Sons, 2004) documents some others such as catering to an aging demographic, or investing by the sea, that can also be relied upon to give better than average results. Using several strategies simultaneously compounds the effects, such as investing in an assisted-living facility by the sea in a fast-growth city.

When you consider the tremendous advantages of real estate, and combine them with the low-tax environment of an IRA, you will understand why using your IRA to invest in real estate makes such a lot of sense (and money).

Conclusion

A ccording to Forbes, 75 percent of Americans who have reached the age of 50 have no more than $5,000 saved towards their retirement. While it is smartest to begin saving for retirement at an early age, it does not occur to most young people to do so usually because they suffer from delusions of immortality and infallibility, or they simply don't stop to think about it. Many people, once they have entered their forties or fifties, feel that it is too late to start.

All these suppositions are wrong. We are not immortal, not infallible, and it is not too late to start if you are already in your forties or older. However, if you are starting late or with a low capital base, you need to take advantage of each and every tool that can accelerate the build up of your retirement fund. For most people, investing in stamp collections, baseball cards, or comic books is not likely to secure a comfortable retirement.

Based on our own experiences and work histories, we can be accused of being biased. It is our firm belief, though, that investing in real estate offers advantages over all other investment vehicles that are dramatic, identifiable, repeatable, measurable and consistent. Anyone wanting to accelerate the build-up of their retirement nest egg should include, if not exclusively focus on, real estate as the preferred mechanism.

One of the tremendous advantages of real estate as an investment vehicle is that it has particularly good tax breaks. Remember from the beginning of this book, that governments levy taxes not just as a means to generate income, but also to shape social policy. The government wants you to invest in real estate, to help provide housing for the needy that they would otherwise have to house (and they know they are not very good at it). Consequently, the tax breaks, concessions, and rebates offered to real estate investors are already very generous.

Furthermore, governments want to encourage you to save for your own retirement (so that they will not be left picking up the tab). As a result, there are also tremendous tax incentives for your IRA. The tax concessions for real estate and IRAs compound each other to make a very effective and tax-efficient system for creating wealth.

By applying the ideas, systems and strategies presented in this book, you can enjoy tax-free (or almost tax-free) investing in real estate, enabling you to build up a significant retirement fund in a relatively short period of time.

There is no time like the present.

What will you do today to help secure a rich retirement?

Frequently Asked Questions

(1) I make too much money to have a Roth. What can I do?

Count your blessings! Then, look into setting up a Solo 401(k) plan with a Solo Roth 401(k) component. These plans have no income limitations and are the best way for high-income earners to finally put real money into a Roth. In 2006, your contribution limits are $15,000 per year ($20,000 if you're over 50) in salary and $29,000 per year in profit-sharing. Your profit-sharing amount can't go into your Solo Roth 401(k) side, but all of your salary contributions can. If you're married and your spouse works in the business as well, he or she can contribute the same amounts. That's up to $40,000 per year in Roth contributions! Two rules here: (1) you'll need to have your own business, with you and your spouse as the only full-time employees, and (2) you can't contribute more salary than you earn in your business.

(2) I don't have a business, what are my options?

If you don't have a business and aren't interested in starting one, you will be more limited in the types of pension plans you use. The Solo 401(k) and Solo Roth 401(k) plans won't be available to you. But you can still start a truly self-directed IRA or Roth IRA, and you can still use an IRA LLC or a Tax-Free LLC in combination with your IRAs to invest in real estate and other "outside-the-box" investments. Bear in mind here that UBIT and UDFI will be a factor with these plans, but would not be if you were using the Solo Roth 401(k) plan.

(3) How do I find a custodian?

Visit our web site, at www.reirallc.com, to see our list of recommended custodians.

(4) How do I find someone who understands how to properly set up an IRA or Tax-Free LLC?

Visit our web site, at www.reirallc.com, to see our list of recommended formation and maintenance service providers.

(5) Can I self-administer my pension?

No. You need to have a third-party administrator hold title to the pension's assets. But you can self-direct your pension in one of two ways. First, you can use a self-directed IRA or Roth IRA, where you will provide your investment instructions to your plan's administrator, who carries them out. The second way is through an IRA LLC or Tax-Free IRA LLC, where you make the investment decisions and your administrator assumes a background role, holding title to the assets and making sure you don't enter into any prohibited transactions or get involved with any disqualified persons.

(6) My stock broker says I can't buy real estate with my plan. You say I can, why?

The most common reason for seeking different advice is knowledge. Your broker simply may not know about these additional opportunities. Remember, most brokers are trained in a very traditional line of investments—securities, stocks, bonds, promissory notes, mutual funds, shares in publicly traded companies, and so on. These are all investments where brokers and brokerage houses can make a clear and simple profit. Real estate is different. It's not an area where an investment broker can make a profit, so it may not be an area that your broker, or the firm that he or she works for, has explored. Talk to your broker about real estate—in fact, why not give your broker a copy of this book? Brokers who understand and embrace this new style of pension investing will have clients beating a path to their doors in the coming years.

(7) What is the deal on tax when my plan takes out a mortgage to buy property? How can I avoid it?

It's all about tax—the IRS wants to make sure it can tax every dime it can. If your pension takes out a loan to buy a property, the income or gain earned from that property is due in part to untaxed money that wasn't originally yours—it's not coming from your deferred-tax contributions (with a deferred tax plan)—nor is it coming from money that has already been taxed (Roths and Solo Roth 401(k)s). So if you buy a property with 50 percent cash from your pension and a mortgage for the remaining 50 percent, as far as the government is concerned only 50 percent of the money that property generates is due entirely to your pension's investment. The other 50 percent of the profit was generated from money that comes from an outside source, and is fair game for tax.

If you want to avoid taxes entirely in this situation you can—by using either a Solo 401(k) or a Solo Roth 401(k) plan to invest with. Remember, Section 514 of the IRS Code says that a 401(k) plan isn't subject to these taxes.

(8) If I invest pension money in a PPM and the business it invested in later takes out a loan, how will I know? Will it impact me? How do I report it if it does?

First of all, the only time a business loan might affect your pension fund is if your pension invested in a flow-through entity, like a partnership or an LLC. These businesses flow their profits, losses and other tax-related income information through to their owners on something called a Schedule K-1, which is prepared as a part of their yearly tax return. You'll know if there is a loan that impacts your pension because that loan will be reported on the Schedule K-1 that's issued to your pension, and will then be passed through and processed on your pension's tax return.

(9) Are there any other tax issues I should be aware of before I invest pension money into a business?

If a business your pension has invested in produces or sells goods, or provides services, the income it makes will probably be subject to UBIT. Your pension's pro-rata share of that income will be subject to tax at the trust income tax rate. If that business obtained a loan to start or keep operating, your pension may also have to pay UBIT over the portion of the business's income that was earned because it incurred the debt.

Sometimes, you'll need to report certain business investments that your Roth IRA or your Tax-Free LLC (funded by your Solo Roth 401(k) plan makes. Typically, these are transactions made between a business that is largely owned by a Roth IRA or Tax-Free LLC and another business that is also owned or run by the Roth IRA or Tax-Free LLC owners. These types of transactions are called "listed" transactions. They aren't illegal or prohibited, but you do need to give the IRS notice when you enter into one.

If you're not sure if a transaction might be considered a prohibited transaction, open a separate self-directed IRA account to make the investment. That way, the worst thing that can happen is you might end up having to pay tax on the amount that is invested in that particular venture. You won't put all of your main pension investments at risk for tax.

(10) I want to start my own business that I will operate. Can I use my pension money as start-up capital?

Not usually. The IRS doesn't want to see you personally receive any direct benefit from an investment made by your pension plan. Starting up your own business means that you personally will receive some type of benefit—a salary, profit-sharing, and so forth, and that makes this a difficult fit in the eyes of the IRS. You could take out a loan against your plan, however.

(11) I want to invest in a start-up business along with my brother and my dad. Now can I use my pension money as start-up capital?

If you were interested in starting up a business where you were a passive investor, things change. If you were to start up this business, along with relatives, either those considered disqualified persons (parents, grandparents, children) or qualified (brothers, sisters, aunts, uncles, cousins), and everyone invests at the same time—including your pension fund—it may be possible. But this is *not* something you want to even try without talking to a knowledgeable attorney and your pension administrator first.

(12) Can I invest my pension into a company that I only own a portion of?

Yes, depending on your ownership percentage and the ownership percentage of any other disqualified persons. If you own 25 percent of a company and your wife, parents and children don't own more than an additional 24 percent between them, then you can bring your pension fund in. But if you and your family were to own 50 percent or more of that company, then you won't be able to bring your pension money in.

(13) Why would I pay UBIT on investments made into a business but not on investments I make into real estate?

Because the goods or services produced through the business are not being created for the sole benefit of your pension—they're being created for the purposes of making money for the business. An investment into a piece of real estate is for the sole benefit of your pension—its only purpose is to make money for your pension. But a business exists to make money for itself first, and then to share that money with its shareholders. Remember also, if your pension were to take out a mortgage for any real estate investments held in your pension, then a portion of your earnings from that real estate investment would become subject to UBIT.

If you wanted to invest in a business and avoid UBIT, make sure the business is run through a C Corporation. C Corporations are not subject to UBIT, because they pay tax on their earnings at a corporate income tax rate.

(14) Who should consider a self-directed pension plan?

A self-directed IRA is a good fit for people who want their retirement fund to grow faster than it would with traditional plans. It's also a good fit for real estate investors who want to turn their investments into even more tax-advantaged operations by running them through something like a Solo Roth 401(k) Plan, combined with a Tax-Free LLC.

But it's important that you have some investment knowledge to begin with, or are prepared to do what it takes to educate yourself. If you are a complete investing novice, then it will be much harder for you to make money, and you run a much higher risk of making some bad investment decisions that will hurt you down the road.

(15) Who should not consider a self-directed pension plan?

If you don't have the time or energy to educate yourself about investing in general, this may not be a good fit for you. You may be safer in a traditional type of plan with someone else at the reins. Your returns may be smaller, but at least you'll have some.

Likewise, if you're a determined do-it-yourselfer, intent on doing everything yourself without input from anyone else, this may not work. Remember, to make a self-directed pension plan truly work you'll need a good custodian (who you actively consult with and listen to) and you'll need help from an attorney or experienced formation service to make sure you form the right type of IRA or Tax-Free LLC. Otherwise, you're a prohibited transaction just waiting to happen.

(16) I want to buy a vacation property. I'm planning to rent it out most of the time, and only plan to use it for about one week per year. Can my pension fund buy this property?

No. Because if the vacation property is owned 100 percent by your pension fund, it is what's called a "plan asset." You, as the owner of your pension fund, cannot make any personal use of a plan asset. Even though you'd only be using the property for a very small period of time, even one day is enough to taint the property for your pension.

(17) I want to set up an IRA LLC. I live in Montana but will be operating real estate rentals in more than one state. Where should I set up the LLC?

That depends. As a rule it's a good idea to set up an LLC in the state where the property is located. That gives you legal standing in the state, which you may need if you get some bad tenants and have to take them to court. But if you have property in more than one state, you have a couple of options. You can (a) register one LLC to do business in each state where it owns property, or you can (b) set up separate LLCs in each state. From a liability perspective, Choice (b) can be preferable. If you have lots of properties in your LLC and your LLC is targeted for a lawsuit by an angry tenant, all of the properties in the LLC are theoretically at risk. And, as IRA LLCs typically have to put more money down on properties, it's likely there will be more equity at risk.

(18) I want to set up a Tax-Free LLC and act as the manager. One of the things the LLC will own is a restaurant. What business activities can I do that won't negatively impact my pension plan or cause me to have a prohibited transaction?

As the manager of an IRA LLC or a Tax-Free LLC, you are allowed to carry out managerial tasks. So you can hire people, fire people, maintain books and business records, and make business-related decisions. But you can't take a salary for your efforts, nor could the restaurant pay you any type of performance bonuses.

(19) I have a self-directed IRA that owns real estate. To whom do my tenants make their rent checks payable?

If you are operating through a plan custodian, then your tenants would make their rent checks payable to the pension fund.

They can send their checks to you, or directly to your custodian. If you are running an apartment building through a property management service, the rent checks would be collected and forwarded to your plan custodian by the property management company. *Under no circumstances should you deposit a rent check into your personal account, even if it is made out to you.* You can't turn around and write a check to your pension, nor can you endorse the rent check. You'll need to ask your tenants to submit a new check with the proper payee's name on it.

(20) I have an IRA LLC that owns real estate. To whom do my tenants make their rent checks payable?

In this case, your LLC owns the property directly, so your tenants would make their rental checks payable either to your IRA LLC or to a property management company, if you are using one. But again, you should never accept a check made payable to you personally, nor should you either endorse it or deposit it and write your LLC a replacement check. All of these things will get you into a mess with the IRS.

(21) I have an IRA LLC that owns a rental property. I want to put a new roof on the property. Can I do that without any negative consequences to my pension fund?

No. You are limited to managerial functions only—hiring and firing subcontractors, property management companies or yard service companies, and making management decisions like when to remodel or sell the property. Once you start doing work that adds value to the property—putting on a new roof, or doing the remodeling yourself—the IRS will consider you to be making illegal contributions to your pension fund.

(22) I want to buy a dress shop with my IRA LLC. I'll own half, and my sister will own the other half. I'm going to be putting up the purchase price of $75,000 through my pension fund, and my sister is going to run the shop as her contribution. How will my pension fund get its money back?

One thing to remember is that your pension fund isn't lending the LLC money to buy the dress shop. Your pension fund is investing in the LLC, which then takes that money to invest in real estate, businesses or other investments. You will get your money back through profit distributions from the LLC, or through the subsequent sale of the dress shop. It's just like investing in a mutual fund—you hope your mutual fund makes money and issues dividends. If it doesn't, the only way you can make your money back is to sell your mutual funds. And if your mutual funds or your dress shop have declined in value, you lose the difference between what you originally invested and what you were able to sell the asset for.

(23) Can I lend my relatives down payment money from my self-directed IRA or my Tax-Free LLC?

Yes! Your pension or your IRA LLC can lend money to anyone who isn't a disqualified person (that's you, your spouse, your parents, grandparents and children, or your spouse's parents, grandparents or children, your plan's custodian, and a few others). Make sure the loan is properly secured with some type of collateral and consider getting some advice or assistance from a knowledgeable attorney or your plan custodian ahead of time.

(24) What does "nonrecourse" mean and why is that the only type of loan my bank is prepared to offer my pension fund?

"Nonrecourse" means that the lender can't come after you for anything other than the property it loaned you money to buy. It can't try to attack any of your pension's other assets, or try to collect from you personally. Because of this, the bank wants to make sure you have some serious money sunk into the deal, as that makes you a better financial risk.

(25) Would you suggest using pension money to invest in a property that is cash-flow negative but has great appreciation potential?

That definitely depends on your own risk tolerance. If you can't rent the property out at a high enough price to make money, you will be draining your pension money each month to make up the difference. Without the opportunity to make money each month, you are limiting your return on investment to that potential appreciation. The biggest risk will be what happens if your pension runs out of money. Remember you usually can't put your own money in without running the risk of having the entire pension investment be targeted as a prohibited transaction.

Index

Meet Diane Kennedy

Diane Kennedy, the nation's preeminent tax strategist, is owner of Diane Kennedy & Associates, a leading tax strategy and accounting firm, and founder of Tax Loopholes.com, a tax education company. Diane is the author of *The Wall Street Journal* and *BusinessWeek* best sellers *Loopholes of the Rich* and *Real Estate Loopholes*, and co-author of *The Insider's Guide to Real Estate Investing Loopholes*, *The Insider's Guide to Making Money in Real Estate, Tax Loopholes for eBay Sellers*, and *Maui Millionaires*.

Diane's extensive teachings have empowered people throughout the country to minimize their tax liabilities through the use of legal tax loopholes.

Diane has written for numerous financial publications, and has been featured in *Kiplinger's Personal Finance*, *The Wall Street Journal*, and *USA Today*, and on CNN and CNBC.

A highly sought-after international speaker and educator, she has dedicated her career to empowering and educating others about financial investments and the tax advantages that are available. Through Diane's knowledge and execution of tax loopholes in her business and real estate investments, she and her husband Richard are able to contribute to special life-changing projects and charities in the United States and around the world.

For the latest expert advice on tax loopholes and critical tax law updates, as well as wealth-building resources, visit her web site: www.taxloopholes.com.

Meet Dolf de Roos

Dr. Dolf de Roos began investing in real estate as an undergraduate student. Despite going on to earn a Ph.D. in electrical and electronic engineering from the University of Canterbury, Dolf increasingly focused on his flair for real estate investing, which has enabled him to have never had a job. He has, however, invested in many classes of real estate (residential, commercial, industrial, hospitality, and specialist) all over the world.

Today he is the chairman of the public company Property Ventures Limited, an innovative real estate investment company whose stated mission is to massively increase stockholders' worth. Over the years, Dolf was cajoled into sharing his investment strategies, and he has run seminars on the Psychology of Creating Wealth and on Real Estate Investing throughout North America, Australia, New Zealand, Asia, the Middle East, and Europe since the 1980s.

Beyond sharing his investment philosophy and strategies with tens of thousands of investors (beginners as well as seasoned experts), Dolf has also trained real estate agents, written and published numerous bestselling books on property, and introduced computer software designed to analyze and manage properties quickly and efficiently. He often speaks at investors' conferences, real estate agents' conventions, and his own international seminars, and regularly takes part in radio shows and television debates. Born in New Zealand, raised in Australia, New Zealand, and Europe, Dolf, with six languages up his sleeve, offers a truly global perspective on the surprisingly lucrative wealth-building opportunities of real estate.

Today, Dolf is a Visiting Professor of Real Estate at the University of North Texas, and teaches at events and institutions in more than 16 countries, including Tony Robbins' Wealth Mastery and Trump University. He appears regularly on TV networks, including CNNfn, NY1, Fox TV, and ABC, and is heard on more than 4,000 radio stations, including NPR and Bloomberg Radio. His weekly video mentoring program is seen in 39 countries.

To find out what you can learn from Dolf's willingness to share his knowledge about creating wealth through real estate, and to receive his free monthly newsletter, please visit his web site at www.dolfderoos.com.